ROWAN LIVING

For Carole O'Toole & Mic Cooper

ROWAN
LIVING

BOOK 1

Thirty projects by Gail Abbott and Jane Bolsover

photography by Mark Scott

A ROWAN PRODUCTION

First published in Great Britain in 2002
by Rowan Yarns
Green Lane Mill, Holmfirth
West Yorkshire, England HD9 2DX

Location manager and Styling: **Gail Abbott**   Photography: **Mark Scott**
Book and Jacket design: **Downes Design**   Illustrations: **Carolyn Jenkins**
Technical illustrations: **Siriol Clarry**   Sub editor: **Natalie Minnis**

British Library Cataloguing-in-Publication Data.
Rowan Yarns
Living Book 1
ISBN 09540949-4-8

Colour reproduction by Chroma Graphics (Overseas) Pte. Ltd
Printed and Bound in Singapore by KHL Printing Co. Pte. Ltd

The Publishers have made every effort to ensure that all instructions given in this book are accurate, but cannot
accept liability for any resulting loss or damage, whether direct or consequential and howsoever arising.

About the Photographer
Mark Scott is a location lifestyle photographer specializing in Interiors, gardens and travel. His relaxed style and
fresh lighting has earned him commissions for numerous UK publications and his work regularly appears in
Magazines such as *Woman & Home*, *Ideal Home* and *House Beautiful*.

Author's Acknowledgements
We would like to thank all those who have given their time and expertise to make this book possible. Especially
Mark Scott for his enthusiasm and skill in giving us beautiful pictures, and for Nicky at Downes Design for
turning our ideas into the finished book.

In addition we would like to thank Lizzie Hutton and Belinda Bamber for letting us use their houses. Thanks
too, to Gaye Hawkins and Beryl Miller who helped us to make the projects, and to Breeze and Quintessential
for loaning us props.

All Drima and Sylko threads, Anchor embroidery threads and Prym sewing aids,
distributed in the UK by Coats Crafts UK, P.O Box 22, Lingfield House, Lingfield Point, McMullen Road,
Darlington, Co. Durham, DL1 1YQ. Consumer helpline: 01325 394237.
Anchor embroidery thread and Coats sewing threads, distributed in the USA by Coats & Clark,
4135 South Stream Blvd, Charlotte, North Carolina 28217. Tel: 704 329 5016. Fax: 704 329 5027.
Prym products distributed in the USA by Prym-Dritz Corp, 950 Brisack Road, Spartanburg, SC 29303.
Tel: +1 864 576 5050, Fax: +1 864 587 3353, e-mail: pdmar@teleplex.net
Breeze: 01223 354403. Quintessential: 01223 525717.

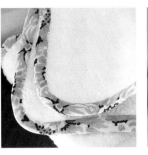

Contents

Biographies

Gail Abbott is an established designer, writer and stylist specialising in interiors, gardens and crafts. Her association with Rowan reaches back to the days when she was editor of the Rowan Journal, helping to bring about the success of Rowan International, so she will be well known to its members around the world. Today Gail writes and styles features regularly for *Rowan Knitting* Magazine, as well as contributing to major UK magazines like *Woman & Home*, *Country Homes and Interiors*, *Ideal Home* and *Essentials* and many of her craft designs can be seen in the pages of *Make It!* magazine. Gail's personal style has evolved over many years spent scouring junk shops and car boot sales, looking for china and furniture. 'I like to think of it as rescuing unwanted pieces and giving them a new lease of life,' she says. 'It's easy just to go out and buy new items, but I love the way an old coffee jug or battered wicker chair tells its own story.'

Jane Bolsover has over 20 years' experience as a designer and writer, and is currently the editor of UK based *Make It!* magazine and the Sewing editor of *Essentials* magazine. After training originally in Fashion and Design at Leicester, Jane worked for a variety of companies over 11 years, and was given the opportunity to collaborate with leading designers of the time, such as Bill Gibb and Benny Ong. As well as writing for magazines, Jane has written two soft furnishing books, and edited Rowan's first three Patchwork and Quilting books. Besides writing, Jane has also appeared on mainstream television several times demonstrating her talents with textiles, and is about to embark on a new 10 part craft series. She is a regular contributor at major craft exhibitions and has demonstrated for international companies, giving advise on fabrics, soft furnishings and dressmaking. Jane lives in Oxfordshire, England, with her two cats Chloé and Loulou.

Introduction

Welcome to the very first Rowan Living book. You may well be familiar with Rowan's Kaffe Fassett Fabric Collection, which was originally designed for patchwork projects, but we feel the range is so exciting and colourful that we couldn't resist thinking of other ways to use them.

The story behind the fabrics is really fascinating, and one that we love. Renowned artist Kaffe Fassett was asked by the charity Oxfam to advise poverty-stricken weaving villages in India on designs that could be marketed in the West. The result is a range of beautiful stripes, checks and plain fabrics, all individually woven on simple hand looms. Being hand-woven, this means that no two fabrics are identical, and the small imperfections that occur in the process only add to the inherent beauty of these cloths. The Indian fabrics perfectly compliment Kaffe's multi-coloured floral prints, and the combination of the two makes for very exciting design possibilities.

Originally our idea was to come up with 25 designs for bedding, table linen and soft curtains, but once we got started we just couldn't stop. We've worked together for many years, but we felt this book was a unique opportunity for us to collaborate and pool our different talents and skills. Together, we've designed accessories for every room in the house, from oven gloves and a pinny for the kitchen, to a Zen shower curtain and rag rug for the bathroom. There's even some simple accessories for the garden, like night light holders and a colourful banner, so let's hope for a long, hot summer so we can all enjoy them.

It was a treat to go on location to France last summer, where half the projects were photographed at a beautiful old farmhouse deep in the Aveyron countryside. The light was perfect, and it was just the place for eating breakfast on the terrace, and having a late drink as the sun went down after a hard day's shoot! The remainder of the book was shot in England in one of our favourite houses in East Anglia. With its 'fifties-style' kitchen and hand-built bathroom, all we needed was for photographer Mark Scott to work his magic.

We hope you have as much pleasure making up the projects as we had designing them. We've included something for everyone, from beginners to the more experienced among you, but all of the ideas are easily achievable. So whether you go along with our suggested colourways, or decide on your own combinations to suit your home, we're sure you'll have lots of fun.

Gail Abbott   Jane Bolsover

TERRACE AND GARDEN

Summer is the time to spend every available moment outside, from a leisurely early breakfast with coffee and croissants to a late glass of wine with friends as the sun goes down. Make the most of outdoor living with simple, stylish makes whether you have acres of green lawn or just a tiny courtyard.

Breakfast on the Terrace
Egg cosy

MATERIALS FOR ONE EGG COSY
- Two 12cm (4⅝in) squares of Narrow Check (NC 03)
- Two 12cm (4⅝in) squares of lightweight batting
- 33cm (13in) of 2.5cm- (1in-) wide bias binding in Persimmon Shot Cotton (SC 07), see 'Making bias binding' in the Technique know-how, on page 61
- Matching threads
- Fade away fabric marker pen, or chalk pencil

TO MAKE

1 Lay the batting pieces on to a flat surface and lay the checked fabric on top of the batting. Pin and baste the layers together around the outer edges. Working on the batting side, draw parallel diagonal lines spaced 3cm (1¼in) apart across each egg cosy piece. Turn the pieces 90 degrees and draw parallel lines spaced as before in the opposite direction, to form a diamond grid. Machine quilt along the drawn lines.

2 Trace over the egg cosy template printed on page 71, and use template to cut out a cosy shape from each quilted square.

3 Cut a 6cm (2⅜in) length from the bias binding and press in half lengthways with the turnings inside. Stitch pressed edges together. Fold in half to make a loop and stitch the raw ends to the right side of one egg cosy piece, placing it at the centre of the curved edge at the notch position marked on the template.

4 Machine stitch the two cosy pieces, right sides together, along one side, for a distance of 5cm (2in) up from the straight edges, with a 6mm (¼in) seam allowance.

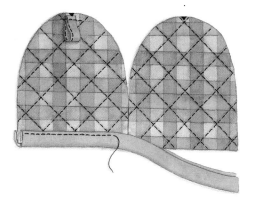

5 Open out the two joined cosy pieces and neaten the straight joined edge by applying bias binding folded in half lengthways with turnings inside and machine stitched over the raw edge. Stitch the remaining curved edges of the cosy, right sides together, with a 6mm (¼in) seam allowance, keeping the lower bound edges level and sandwiching the loop in place at the top. Neaten turnings together and turn egg cosy to right side.

Placemat

MATERIALS FOR ONE PLACEMAT
- 35.5 x 48cm (14 x 19in) of Jewel Damask (GP 02-J) for the top
- 35.5 x 48cm (14 x 19in) of Persimmon Shot Cotton (SC 07) for the backing
- 35.5 x 48cm (14 x 19in) of lightweight batting
- 1.5m (1⅝yd) of 2.5cm- (1in-) wide bias binding in Persimmon Shot Cotton (SC 07), see 'Making bias binding' in the Technique know-how, on page 61
- Matching threads
- Fade away fabric marker pen, or chalk pencil

TO MAKE

1 On a flat surface, lay out the backing fabric wrong side up, place the batting fabric on top and then the damask fabric, right side up. Smooth out the layers to remove any wrinkles, then pin the layers together at the corners and mid points of each side. Baste layers together close to the edge.

2 Working on the backing side, draw parallel diagonal lines spaced 3cm (1¼in) apart across the fabric. Turn the mat 90 degrees and draw parallel lines spaced as before in the opposite direction, to form a diamond grid. Machine quilt through all the layers of fabric along the drawn lines.

3 Lay the quilted fabric face down and use the base of a cup or mug to draw a curve at each corner. Trim the fabric away at corners to form smooth curves.

Right: What could be more relaxing than breakfast on the terrace with this stylish collection of table accessories? Using jewel colours you can quilt a placemat, keep a cafetiere warm, shape an egg cosy, protect your juice from summer bugs and make a napkin

4 Finish the fabric edges with bias binding, folded in half lengthways with turnings inside and machine stitched over the raw edges. For a neat finish to the bias binding, press the ends 1cm (⅜in) to the wrong side and butt them up close together. Remove any basting stitches that still show.

Cafetiere cover

MATERIALS
- 18 x 30.5cm (7 x 12in) of Jewel Damask (GP 02-J)
- 18 x 30.5cm (7 x 12in) of Persimmon Shot Cotton (SC 07)
- 18 x 30.5cm (7 x 12in) of lightweight batting
- 2.3m (2½yds) of 2.5cm- (1in-) wide bias binding in Persimmon Shot Cotton (SC 07), see 'Making bias binding' in the Technique know-how, on page 61
- Matching threads
- Fade away fabric marker pen, or chalk pencil

TO MAKE
1 Make the main part of the cover following steps 1, 2, 3 and 4 of the placemat. Then, fold the remaining length of bias binding in half lengthways with the turnings inside, stitch the pressed edges together and cut into four equal lengths.

2 Wrap the cover around the cafetiere and mark the positions below the top and above the base of the handle for the ties. Knot one end of each tie to neaten and press the other end 1cm (⅜in) to the wrong side.

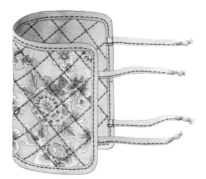

Stitch the pressed ends of each tie to the edge binding on the backing side of the cover at the positions marked.

Napkin

MATERIALS FOR ONE NAPKIN
- 42 x 42cm (16½ x 16½in) square of Narrow Check (NC 03)
- Matching thread

TO MAKE
Press a double turned 1cm (⅜in) hem to the wrong side along each edge of the napkin and machine stitch in place.

Jug cover

MATERIALS
- 23 x 23cm (9 x 9in) square of Narrow Check (NC 03)
- Selection of wooden beads in bright colours
- Matching thread

TO MAKE
1 Press and baste a double turned 1cm (⅜in) hem to the wrong side along each edge of the cover and machine stitch in place. Remove basting stitches.

2 Thread a needle with a length of doubled thread and knot the ends together. Make a small stitch through one of the corners of the fabric square and thread on three beads of different sizes. Pass the needle around the last bead and thread it up through the centre of the first two beads. Fasten thread off with a few stitches through the fabric to secure beads in place. Repeat for the remaining corners.

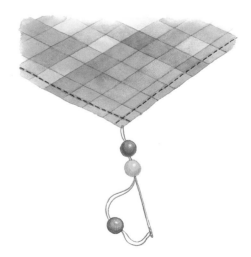

Bring a riot of colour into your garden this summer, with these very easy Celebration banners.
Simply cut with pinking shears and tie them up high in a tree

Celebration banners

MATERIALS
■ Approximately 53 x 75cm (21 x 29½in) of brightly
coloured fabric for each pennant - we used
Alternate Stripes AS 03 and AS 21; Narrow Check
NC 03; Pachrangi Stripe PS 22; Red Roman Glass
GP 01-R; and Persimmon (SC 07) and
Pomegranate (SC 09) Shot Cottons
■ A long length of string
■ Pinking shears
■ Matching thread

TO MAKE
Scale up the pennant template on page 72 and cut out
the number of pennants you require using pinking
shears. Fold over the short top edge of each pennant
2.5cm (1in) and machine stitch in place to form a
channel. Thread the pennants on to your length of
string, alternating the fabric designs and colours. Tie
the ends of the string to high tree branches, or house
drainpipes, to 'fly' your banners.

Reminiscent of days gone by, this distinctive Retro peg bag will brighten up the dullest washdays

Roman glass peg bag

MATERIALS
- 70cm (¾yd) of 114cm- (45in-) wide Circus Roman Glass (GP 01-C) for main bag
- 1.9m (2yds) of 2.5cm- (1in-) wide bias binding in Pine Shot Cotton (SC 21), see 'Making bias binding' in the Technique know-how, on page 61
- Matching threads
- Wooden coathanger
- Hacksaw
- Sandpaper

TO MAKE
1 Using a photocopier scale up the peg bag template on page 71, as indicated on the page. Using the full sized template, cut out two front bags and two back bags from Roman Glass fabric.

2 With right sides facing, stitch the two front pieces together around the central 'window' with a 1cm (⅜in) seam allowance. Clip into the seam turnings and turn to right side. Carefully press seam around the 'window' making sure that the seam is lying right on the edge. Keeping raw edges level, baste the outer edges of the fronts together.

3 With wrong sides facing, and raw edges level, place the two back pieces on top of each other. Place the joined front pieces on top of the back pieces and then baste all the layers together around the outer edges. Finish the fabric edges with bias binding, folded in half lengthways with turnings inside. Start and finish the binding at the top notch position, by pressing the binding ends 1cm (⅜in) to the wrong side and butting them up close together. Stitch binding in place close to the inner edges. Reverse stitching at the start and finish to reinforce. Remove any basting stitches that still show.

4 Using the template as a guide, trim the wooden coathanger down to size using the hacksaw. Sandpaper the ends smooth. Slip coathanger through front 'window' and wiggle the metal hook section out through the binding joint at the top of the bag.

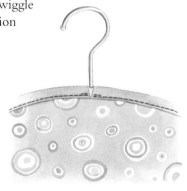

5 To finish, make a bow for the top by pressing the remaining bias binding in half lengthways with the turnings inside and stitching the pressed edges together. Tuck short raw ends inside the binding 'tube' to neaten, then fold the binding strip in half to find central point. Handstitch centre of binding to peg bag binding close to hook, and tie binding into a bow at the front around the hook.

Night Light holders

MATERIALS
- 33 x 75cm (13 x 29½in) of brightly coloured fabric for each holder, cut out using pinking shears – we used Alternate Stripe AS 21; Broad Check BC 02; Red Roman Glass GP 01-R; and Persimmon (SC 07) and Pine (SC 21) Shot Cottons
- Matching thread
- Silver sand or gravel
- Night lights

TO MAKE

1 Fold a piece of fabric in half widthways and stitch the long edges together with a 1.5cm (⅝in) seam allowance to make a bag shape. Open out the bag and squash each base corner flat. Stitch across corners at right angles to side seams, about 5cm (2in) in from the point, to form a small triangle at each base corner (see diagram right).

2 Roll the top edge of the bag outwards a few times to form a cuff around the top. Place bag in position and fill with silver sand or gravel almost to the top and insert a night light in the centre of the sand.

> **WARNING:**
> Never leave burning candles unattended.

Bring candlelight into your garden and you'll be able to linger long after the sun goes down

KITCHEN AND DINING

Greet friends and family with the smell of home baking and make your kitchen the heart of the home with co-ordinated accessories in pastel fabrics. Soft florals, faded stripes and an easy appliqué leaf design evoke the mood of the 1950s with their muted shades of duck egg blue, pink and grey.

The latest look for Roman blinds is to pull the fabric up in less formal folds, doing away with the battens, and creating a much softer feel

Pull up blind

MATERIALS
- Duck Egg Shot Cotton (SC 26) 114cm- (45in-) wide, see below for estimating quantity
- Matching thread
- Small plastic rings (two for each fold)
- Touch-and-close tape to fit width of finished blind
- Fine cord
- 2.5 x 5cm (1 x 2in) timber support to fit width of window recess
- Five large screw eyes
- Toggle end and cleat

ESTIMATING THE FABRIC QUANTITY
Prepare your timber support as shown in the Technique know-how, on page 59 and fix in place. Measure your window to find the finished width and length of the blind, see 'Measuring up for curtains and blinds' in the Technique know-how section, page 57. Add 12cm (5in) to the length and width measurements for hem allowances. This blind is best made from one piece of fabric, but if your window is larger and you need to join fabric widths, allow for a full width to be placed centrally, with part-widths of equal dimensions joined down each side.

TO MAKE
1 Cut out the required number of fabric drops and join the widths together, if necessary, with flat fell seams (see the Technique know-how section on page 61). Press a double 3cm (1¼in) hem down each side edge and machine stitch in place. Turn and press a double 5cm (2in) hem along the lower edge and stitch in place as before. Slipstitch (see the Technique know-how section on page 63) the open ends of the base hem together at the sides.

2 Measure the finished length of the blind from the base hem and mark the top edge of the blind with pins. Press the top hem to the wrong side along the pin-line. Trim the hem allowance to 1.5cm (⅝in) and baste in place. Pin the fluffy side of the touch-and-close tape to the wrong side of the blind at the top, enclosing the raw edge. Machine stitch the tape in place. Remove basting stitches.

3 Work out the fold spacing for the ring positions along each side hem and mark with pins. To do this, place the top rings approximately 36cm (14in) from the top; the base rings at the top of the lower hem, and space the remaining rings approximately 20cm (8in) apart. Hand sew the plastic rings to the inner edges of the side hems at each position marked.

4 Measure 36cm (14in) from the top of the window recess down each side of the window (this should be the same as the distance from the top of your blind to the top rings), and mark with a pencil. If your window has a wooden frame then screw an eye into each side at the positions marked, keeping them as close as possible to the sides of the window recess. If not attach a small piece of timber to each side of the window first, and then screw in the eyes.

5 Fasten the top edge of the blind to the support, using the touch-and-close tape. Working from the underside of the blind, knot a length of cord to each of the bottom rings and thread the cords up through the rest of the rings. Thread each cord through the side screw eyes, then pass them directly up through the eyes in the wooden batten, pass the cord at the left hand side across the top of the blind, so that both

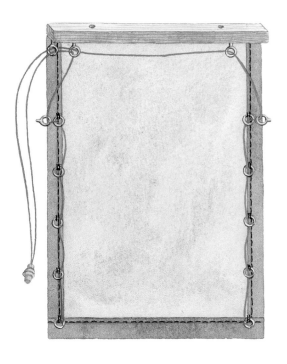

cords pass through the two eyes at the right hand side, of the timber support. Trim the cords so they are level and attach a toggle to prevent them slipping back through the screw eyes.

6 Screw the cleat to the side of the window frame, so that you can secure the cords firmly in place when the blind is raised. Try to make sure that the cleat is not visible when the blind is raised.

Basic striped cushion

MATERIALS
■ 50cm (⅝yd) of 114cm- (45in-) wide Blue Ombre Stripe (OS 02)
■ Matching thread
■ 45 x 45cm (18 x 18in) cushion pad

Cut out one front cushion 48 x 48cm (19 x 19in), one small back 31 x 48cm (12 x 19in), and one larger back 34 x 48cm (13½ x 19in). Turn to the Technique know-how section on page 62, to complete the cushion.

The most basic cushion shape looks fantastic made in this delicately shaded Ombre Stripe

Add a touch of personal panache to your dining room with your own designer table linen. Simple machine appliqué leaves can turn a plain tablecloth into something really special

Appliqué tablecloth and napkins

Finished tablecloth size: 175 x 270cm (69 x 106in)
Finished napkin size: 42 x 42cm (16½ x 16½in)

MATERIALS
■ 2.8m (3yds) of 114cm- (45in-) wide Grass (SC 27) Shot Cotton
■ 30cm (12in) of 114cm- (45in-) wide Duck Egg (SC 26) and Blush (SC 28) Shot Cottons
■ 90cm (1yd) of 45cm- (18in-) wide paper-backed fusible web
■ Matching threads

TO MAKE
1 For the tablecloth, cut one central panel 112 x 260cm (44 x 102in) and two side panels 33.5 x 260cm (13¼ x 102in) in Grass Shot Cotton. From the remaining Grass fabric cut six napkins 46 x 46cm (18 x 18in) each.

2 With right sides facing, seam the two side panels to the central panel along the long edges with a French seam (see Technique know-how, page 60). Press a double turned 12mm (½in) hem to the wrong side

along each edge of the tablecloth and machine stitch in place.

3 Press a double turned 1cm (⅜in) hem to the wrong side along each side edge of the napkins and machine stitch the hems in place.

4 Using a hot iron, stick half of the paper-backed fusible web to the wrong side of the Duck Egg fabric, and the remainder to the Blush fabric. Trace off the leaf template on page 73. Using the template, draw 25 leaves on to the paper backing side of each fabric and cut them all out.

5 Remove the paper backing from each leaf shape and place one Blush coloured leaf on three of the napkins and one Duck Egg on the remaining three. Position each leaf diagonally in one corner, leaving plenty of room for the stem. Press the leaves in place using the hot iron.

6 Set your sewing machine to a medium sized, close zigzag stitch and, using either matching or contrasting thread, stitch around the edges of the leaves, enclosing all the raw edges.

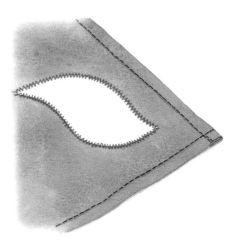

7 Draw a long curve from the base of the leaf with a pencil, as shown on the template for the stem. Stitch over the line with zigzag stitch, setting it very narrow for a few stitches then gradually widening out to full width for the remainder of the stem.

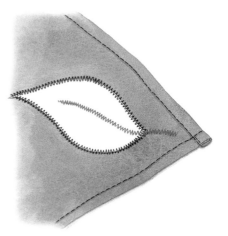

8 Appliqué the remaining leaves on to the edges of the tablecloth in the same manner, placing them 8cm (3in) in from the edges, approximately 10cm (4in) apart, and alternating the colours.

Appliqué matching napkins to complete the set.

Country Pinny

MATERIALS
- 1.3m (1½yds) of 114cm- (45in-) wide Stone Forget-me-not Rose (GP 08-S)
- Matching thread
- Large piece of paper

TO MAKE

1 Scale up the pinny front and pocket pattern pieces on to the large piece of paper, as indicated on page 74. Using the full sized pattern pieces, cut out one pinny front, and one pocket. From the remaining fabric cut two straight grain strips 7.5 x 94cm (3 x 37in) for waist ties, and one 7.5 x 65cm (3 x 25½in) for the neck strap.

2 Using an overlock machine, zigzag stitch or hand overcast stitch (see Technique know-how, on page 63), neaten the two curved edges of the pinny front. Press neatened edges 1cm (⅜in) to wrong side and machine stitch in place.

3 Press a double turned 1cm (⅜in) hem to wrong side down the two long straight side edges of the pinny and machine stitch in place. Press a double 2.5cm (1in) hem to the wrong side along the top and base edges, and machine stitch in place.

4 Press a double turned 1cm (⅜in) hem to wrong side along the straight top edge of the pocket. Machine stitch in place. Press a 1cm (⅜in) single hem to wrong side along curved edge of pocket and baste

in place. With right sides up, lay the pocket centrally on to right side of pinny with the top straight edge lying parallel and 35.5cm (14in) down from top edge of the pinny. Baste and then top stitch in place around the curved edge, with two rows of machine stitching spaced 6mm (¼in) apart. Remove all of the basting stitches.

5 Fold waist ties in half lengthways with right sides facing and machine stitch the long edges together and across one short end with a 1cm (⅜in) seam allowance. Trim corners and turn to right side with the help of a pointed object such as a knitting needle. Press flat, making sure the seamlines lie right on the edges, for a neat finish.

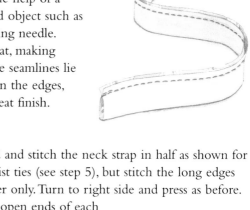

6 Fold and stitch the neck strap in half as shown for the waist ties (see step 5), but stitch the long edges together only. Turn to right side and press as before. At the open ends of each waist tie and neck strap carefully push the raw edges 1cm (⅜in) to the wrong side, i.e. down inside the 'tubes'. Press and baste edges together.

7 Working on the wrong side, pin the short basted edges of the neck strap to the pinny at the outer edges of the top hem, keeping the ends of the strap level with the base of the hem. Machine stitch in place with a row of 'boxed' stitches, (see diagram above). Attach the waist ties to the top edges of the straight side hems in the same way. Remove basting stitches.

Right: Bring back fond memories of your granny's pinny, the faded tones of Forget-me-not Rose are reminiscent of days gone by

Nothing is more comforting than a spot of home baking, especially when you can use your hand-made oven mitts

Stripy Oven mitts

MATERIALS

- 90cm (1yd) of 114cm- (45in-) wide Blue Ombre Stripe (OS 02)
- 20cm (¼yd) of 114cm- (45in-) wide bump interlining
- 2.3m (2½yds) of 2.5cm- (1in-) wide bias binding in Grass Shot Cotton (SC 27), see 'Making bias binding' in the Technique know-how, on page 61
- Matching thread

TO MAKE

1 From the striped fabric, cut two long rectangles 18 x 80cm (7 x 32in) with stripes running down the length, and one to the same measurements in bump interlining. Using the template printed on page 73, curve off the ends of each rectangle. From the remaining stripe, cut out four hand pockets to the exact shape and size of the template, with the stripes running across each piece.

2 On a flat surface, lay out one of the long rectangles, wrong side up. Place the interlining on top and then the remaining long rectangular piece, right side up. Smooth out the layers to remove any wrinkles, then pin and baste the layers together close to the edges.

3 Cut a 10cm (4in) length from the bias binding and press in half lengthways with the turnings inside. Stitch pressed edges together. Fold strip in half to make a loop and stitch the raw ends of the bias binding to the central point of one long edge of the basted rectangles.

4 With wrong sides facing, baste two hand pocket pieces together around the outer edges. Finish the straight edge with bias binding, folded in half lengthways with turnings inside and machine stitched over the raw edges. Trim binding level at the side edges. Repeat with remaining two hand pocket pieces.

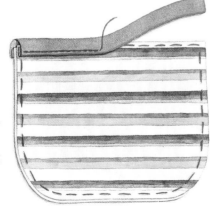

5 Keeping raw edges level, place a bound pocket on each end of the basted long rectangles. Baste pockets in place and finish the edges with bias binding, folded in half lengthways and machine stitched in place. Make sure that you sandwich the pockets and loops in place at the same time. For a neat finish to the bias binding, press ends 1cm (⅜in) to the wrong side and butt them up close together. Finally, remove any basting stitches that still show.

SITTING ROOM

Rich berry colours in a combination of plains, bold checks and exotic florals give a sunny sitting room a rosy glow. Drape a favourite armchair with a dramatic throw, make a no-sew room divider and lampshade, then hang easy three-tone curtains to bring a taste of summer into your home.

This elegant fabric-covered screen is
a very versatile piece of furniture.
Use it to hide away clutter or to add
privacy at a window

Standing screen

MATERIALS FOR THE WOODEN FRAMES
- Six pieces of 19mm (¾in) square, planed finished timber 152cm (60in) long
- Fifteen pieces of 19mm (¾in) square, planed finished timber 36cm (14¼in) long
- Thirty 4.0 x 30mm (No 8 x 1¼in) wood screws
- Drill with a 3mm (⅛in) drill and countersink bit
- Bradawl
- Set square and pencil

TO MAKE

1 Take one of the uprights (the 152cm/60in long timber pieces) and using the set square and pencil, mark the positions for where the five horizontals (the 36cm/14¼in timber pieces) will be attached, as shown. Mark the centre of each position.

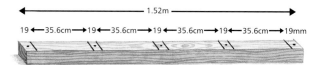

2 To ensure the uprights are marked in exactly the same position, put the one you've marked against a wall and line up the remaining uprights against it. Transfer all the marks by drawing across the remaining five uprights using the pencil and set square, once again marking the centres of each position. It will help if someone holds the wood while you do this.

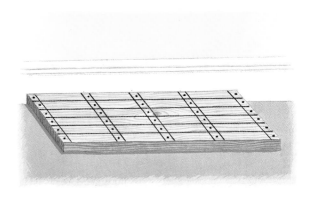

3 Using the bradawl make a hole in the timber at each central position marked along the six uprights (there should be five holes on each upright), and then drill a hole right through the timber at each position. Countersink each drilled hole.

4 Place five horizontals on the floor at right angles to a wall, lining the ends up with an upright's holes. Screw the upright to each horizontal.

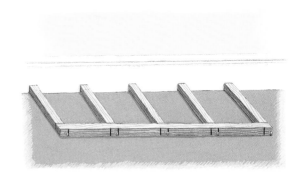

5 Carefully turn the frame around, and place another upright against the opposite ends of the horizontals. Screw this in place. Repeat steps 4 and 5 to make two more identical frames. Line all three frames up together and, using the set square, check to make sure they are all square.

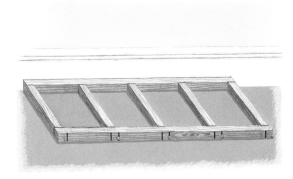

MATERIALS FOR COVERING AND COMPLETING THE SCREEN

MATERIALS
- 5m (5½yds) of 114cm- (45in-) wide of Exotic Check (EC 05)
- 3.10m (3½yds) of 137cm- (54in-) wide bump interlining
- 12m (13¼yd) of 16mm- (⅝in-) wide braid, binding or tape in a toning colour
- Three wooden frames (see left)
- Fabric glue
- Tailor's chalk
- Six 65mm (2½in) butt hinges, in brass
- Thirty six 3.5mm x 20mm (No. 6 x ¾in) brass screws
- Staple gun, or hammer and tacks
- Bradawl

TO MAKE

1 Cut six rectangles of bump interlining 42 x152cm (16½ x 60in). Place one frame on a flat surface and lay one of the bump interlining pieces centrally on top. To secure it in place, start by inserting a holding staple (or tack) on the face side of the top bar of the

frame in the centre. Pull gently on the interlining so that it is taut and secure a holding staple (or tack) at the centre of the bottom bar. Secure the sides in the same way. Fix the interlining in place by spacing staples or tacks, about 12cm (5in) apart, pulling the fabric so it feels firm but not stretched. Repeat to attach another piece of interlining to the other side of the frame. Trim away the excess fabric that overhangs the edges of the frame.

2 Cut out three rectangles of checked fabric, each to fit the size of a single frame, plus an extra 2cm (¾in) hem allowance all round, and then another three panels with an extra 3.5cm (1½in) hem allowance all the way round. The quickest way to do this is to lay the fabric out on the floor, right side up, place a frame on top, and mark the hem allowances round the edge with tailor's chalk. In this way, you can see exactly how the checks will match up on each of the frames before you cut out the fabric.

3 Lay an interlined screen on a flat surface and lay one of the smaller fabric pieces (with smaller hem allowances) centrally on top, right side up. Insert the holding staples or tacks as shown for the interlining in step 1, but insert them into the sides of the frame by wrapping the fabric over the edges, enclosing the interlining completely.

4 Stand the frame upright and fold the fabric over the edge. Making sure that you keep the fabric checks running straight, secure along the top with staples or tacks spacing them 12cm (5in) apart. Do not fasten the corners down yet. Turn the screen the other way up, pulling the fabric once again so it feels firm, but not

stretched. Repeat to attach the fabric at the two sides. Fold the corners neatly and staple or tack in place. Trim away any excess fabric that overhangs at the back of the frame.

5 Lay the frame fabric side down and place one of the larger fabric pieces centrally over the opposite interlined side. Insert the holding staples as shown in step 3. Stand the frame upright once again, and fold the raw fabric edge under along the top edge so that it is flush with the front of the screen. Make sure the checks line up at the sides before you begin, then secure the top edge in place with staples or tacks as described in step 4. Repeat to secure the remaining sides.

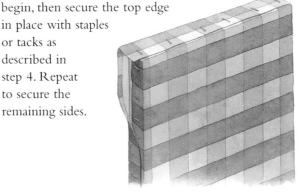

6 To disguise the staples or tacks, attach a length of braid or tape to the outer edges of the panel using the fabric glue. Secure the cut ends in place at the base with a staple or tack. Repeat steps 1 to 6 to cover the two remaining panels.

7 Place two of the covered panels together so that the tops and bases correspond. Mark the positions of the three hinges on one side edge of each screen using the bradawl. Screw the hinges loosely in position and then stand the panels to check the positioning, before tightening the screws. Hinge the remaining panel to the other two, so that the screen concertinas when stood up.

Reversible throw

MATERIALS

- 3.10m (3⅓yds) of 114cm- (45in-) wide Jewel Flower Lattice (GP 11-J)
- 1.8m (2yds) of 150cm- (60in-) wide burgundy coloured fleece
- Matching thread

TO MAKE

1 Cut out two rectangular pieces of Flower Lattice fabric 96.5 x 140cm (38 x 55in). IMPORTANT These two pieces of fabric are to be seamed together down the long edges, to form one piece, so make sure that the patterns will match across the width before you start cutting out. Cut one piece of fleece 122 x 172cm (48 x 58⅝in).

2 With right sides facing, stitch the two Flower Lattice pieces together down one long edge, with a 1.5cm (⅝in) seam allowance. Take care to match up the floral print. Press the seam turnings open.

3 Press a 1.5cm (⅝in) hem to the wrong side around all edges of the print fabric, and then press over another 7.5cm (3in) hem. Lay the print fabric out on a flat surface with the wrong side uppermost and open out the deeper hems. Lay the fleece fabric in the centre of the print fabric with its edges up to the deeper hem press marks. Smooth out the layers to remove any wrinkles. With the pressed hems opened out pin the layers together at the corners and mid points on each side. Baste the two layers together close to the edge of the fleece.

The floral borders are mitred at the corners for a neat professional finish.

4 Fold the deeper hems over on top of the fleece and mitre the corners (see Technique know-how, page 62). Baste the hems in place through all layers of fabric, close to the inner pressed edge. Slipstitch (see Technique know-how, page 63) the mitred corners together, then topstitch the hems in place working close to the edge of the hem. Remove all basting stitches.

Left: Liven up a plain fleece throw by adding a contrasting floral backing and border around the edge

Three tone curtains

MATERIALS

- Three Shot Cotton fabrics, 114cm- (45in-) wide (see below for estimating the quantity). We used Pomegranate (SC 09), Bittersweet (SC 10) and Persimmon (SC 07)
- 7.5cm- (3in)- wide pencil-pleat heading tape, to fit width of ungathered curtain
- Matching threads

ESTIMATING THE FABRIC QUANTITY

Measure your window to find the finished width and length of the curtains (see 'Measuring up for curtains and blinds' in the Technique know-how, page 57). Divide your length measurement into three, then add the following to each of the panel dimensions. Top panel: add 2cm (¾in) to the top edge for the heading, and 1.5cm (⅝in) at the base for a seam allowance. Middle panel: add 1.5cm (⅝in) at the top and base for seam allowances. Lower panel: add 15cm (6in) for the base hem, and 1.5cm (⅝in) at the top edge for a seam allowance.

TO MAKE

1 Cut out the required number of top, middle and lower panels from the three contrasting fabrics. Join fabric widths if necessary to obtain the correct curtain width, with flat fell seams (see the Technique know-how section, on page 61). With right sides facing, join the panels together with French seams (see Technique know-how section, on page 60), to form your full length curtain.

2 Press a double-turned 1.5cm (⅝in) hem along the side edges of the joined fabric, and machine stitch in place. Press a double 7.5cm (3in) hem along the base

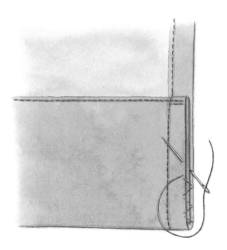

edge, and either machine, or slip hem in place by hand (see Technique know-how, page 63). Slipstitch (see Technique know-how, page 63) together the open side edges of the base hem.

3 Measure the finished curtain length from the base hem and mark with pins. Press over the top edge to the wrong side along the pin-line. Starting at the leading edge, position the heading tape on the wrong side of the curtain, close to the top edge. Fold under about 1.5cm (⅝in) of tape at one end and secure the cords with a knot on the wrong side of the tape. Pin the tape in place. Allowing a further 1.5cm (⅝in) for folding under, cut off the heading tape at the opposite end, and leave the cord ends free.

4 Starting at the lower edge of the tape on the leading edge, machine stitch up the short side, along the top and down the opposite short edge. Starting again at the leading edge, machine stitch along the lower edge of the tape, ensuring that the fabric below is smooth, otherwise the curtain may pucker up when the tape is pulled up.

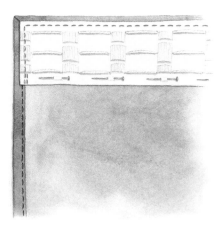

Note: Deep colours may fade in bright sunlight, especially if the curtains are un-lined. We suggest you hang these curtains away from direct bright sunlight, for longer life.

Left: Choose three vibrant shades of plain fabric to make these designer curtains for taller windows and French doors

Laminated lampshade

MATERIALS
- 70cm (¾yd) of 114cm- (45in-) wide Broad Check (BC 04)
- One deep coolie lampshade
- Sticky-backed tie-back and pelmet stiffener
- Strong fabric glue
- Clothes pegs

TO MAKE

1 Carefully remove the cover from the lampshade to use as a pattern. You will probably find that you end up with two separate wire rings, one extending into the bulb holder. Keep them safe to one side for the present. On the paper backing side of the sticky-backed tie-back and pelmet stiffener, draw around the lampshade cover, adding an extra 1.5cm (⅝in) along one of the straight sides. Cut out the shape using sharp scissors.

2 Make sure your fabric is pressed free of creases and lay it out on a flat surface. Peel off the paper backing from the lampshade shape and stick the shape to the fabric, placing one straight edge along a line of checks and taking care not to form creases. Smooth out the fabric firmly with your hand, to make sure it is well stuck down to the stiffener.

3 Trim the fabric to leave a 1.5cm (⅝in) hem allowance around all edges. Then, trim one hem flush to the stiffener along one straight edge. On the other straight edge fold over the hem and stick in place with the fabric glue. Leave to dry.

4 When dry, bring the two straight edges together and overlap them by 1.5cm (⅝in) with the hemmed edge on top. Glue the edges together and hold in place with the pegs until the glue is completely dry.

5 Insert the smaller wire ring inside the top of the new shade, fold over the fabric hem to enclose the ring and glue in place. Use the pegs once again to hold in place until the glue is completely dry. Repeat with the hem and large wire ring at the base to complete the lampshade.

Give a new lease of life to a tired coolie lampshade, with a richly-coloured checked cover

BEDROOM

Make your bedroom a romantic haven
where you can retire and relax away the
strains of the day. Pastel colours and
scented sachets delight the senses, while
pretty floral bedlinen, soft cushions and
casually draped curtains diffuse the light.

Create a feminine bedroom with coordinating bed linen, using a combination of pretty florals and sorbet-coloured plains

Tie fastening bed linen

MATERIALS FOR A SINGLE BED DUVET AND TWO PILLOWCASES
- 4m (4½yds) of 114cm- (45in-) wide Water Melon Shot Cotton (SC 33)
- 4.3cm (4¾yds) of 114cm- (45in-) wide Forget-me-not Rose (GP 08-C)
- Matching thread

MATERIALS FOR A DOUBLE BED DUVET AND TWO PILLOWCASES
- 5m (5½yds) of 114cm- (45in-) wide Water Melon Shot Cotton (SC 33)
- 4.3cm (4¾yds) of 114cm- (45in-) wide Forget-me-not Rose (GP 08-C)
- Matching thread

CUTTING OUT

For a single duvet, from the plain fabric cut: two large backing panels 110 x 130cm (43¼ x 51¼in), one small backing panel 33.5 x 130cm (13¼ x 51¼in), and four ties each 3.5 x 25cm (1⅜ x 10in). From print fabric cut: two front panels 67 x 160cm (26¼ x 63in), making sure that you match the print down the long edges.

For a double duvet, from plain fabric cut: two large backing panels 110 x 196cm (43¼ x 77¼in), one small backing panel 33.5 x 196cm (13¼ x 77¼in) and six ties each 3.5 x 25cm (1⅜ x 10in). From print fabric cut two front panels 100 x 160cm (39¼ x 63in), making sure that you match the print down the long edges.

For each pillowcase, from plain fabric cut: one backing panel 51 x 70.5cm (20 x 27½in) and four ties each 3.5 x 25cm (1⅜ x 10in). From print: cut one front panel 51 x 96.5cm (20 x 38in).

TO MAKE THE DUVET COVER

1 With right sides facing, stitch the two front panels together down one long edge with a 1.5cm (⅝in) seam allowance, making sure you carefully match the design. Neaten turnings together and press to one side. With the seam running vertically up the joined panels, press a double-turned 2cm hem to the wrong side along the top edge and machine stitch in place.

2 With right sides facing, stitch the two larger backing panels together down one long edge with a 1.5cm (⅝in) seam allowance. Neaten turnings together and press to one side. Then, join the smaller backing panel to one of the larger panels, along one long edge. Neaten and press as before. Along the remaining long raw edge of the larger backing panels, press a double-turned 4cm (1½in) hem to the wrong side and machine stitch in place.

3 Press the hemmed edge of the backing panel 53cm (21in) over to the wrong side of the fabric to form the flap. Then fold the flap back over on to the right side along the pressline. Baste the flap in place down both raw side edges. On a large flat surface, lay out the backing and place the printed front panel on top with right sides facing and raw edges level. The top hem on the printed front should overlap the hem on the backing flap. Baste and then machine stitch the panels together around the three raw edges with a 1.5cm (⅝in) seam allowance. Neaten turnings together and turn cover through to right side. Press seamed edges flat and remove basting stitches.

4 Fold each tie in half lengthways with right sides facing and machine stitch the long edges and across one short end with a 6mm (¼in) seam allowance. Trim corners and turn through to right side with the help of a pointed object such as a knitting needle. Press flat, making sure seamlines lie right on the edges for a neat finish. Press raw ends of each tie 1cm (⅜in) to the wrong side.

5 Working along the hem of the plain flap, measure and mark with pins the positions of four ties for a single duvet, spaced 25cm (10in), and six for a double, spacing the outer two 33cm (13in) from the edges and the remaining 25cm (10in) apart. Place the raw pressed edge of each tie under the hem at

the positions marked. Pin and baste in place. Machine stitch basted ends of ties with a row of 'boxed' stitches (see diagram below).

6 Lay the duvet out on a large surface and smooth out to make sure that the flap is lying flat. At each tie position, mark the corresponding tie positions, using pins on the printed front. Making sure you stitch through the front layer of fabric only, pin, baste and machine stitch the remaining ties to the front of the cover as shown before.

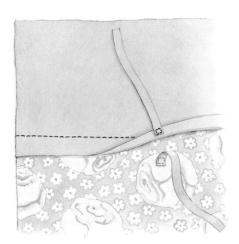

TO MAKE A PILLOWCASE
1 On the front panel, press a double-turned 2cm (¾in) hem to the wrong side along one short end and machine stitch in place. On the backing panel, press a double-turned 4cm (1½in) hem to the wrong side along one short end and machine stitch in place. Fold and press this same edge 15cm (6in) over to the wrong side to form the flap.

2 Fold the flap back over on to the right side of the fabric along the pressline and baste in place down both raw side edges. On a flat surface, lay out the backing and place the front panel on top with right sides together and raw edges level. The top hem on the front should overlap the hem on the backing flap. Baste and then machine stitch the panels together around the three raw edges with a 1.5cm (⅝in) seam allowance. Neaten the seam turnings together and turn the pillowcase through to right side. Press all seamed edges flat.

3 Make up four ties and attach to the pillowcase flap and front as shown in steps 4, 5 and 6 of the duvet cover, placing them 12.5cm (5in) in from each side edge.

The opening at the front gives these pillowcases unusual styling, while the narrow ties are an attractive touch

Beaded throw curtains

MATERIALS

- Blush Shot Cotton (SC 28) 114cm- (45in-) wide (see below for estimating quantity)
- Matching thread
- A selection of pink beads. We used a 6mm (¼in) round bead, a leaf-shaped bead and a tiny bugle bead, for each position (the quantity of beads will depend on the finished width of your curtain – see step 3)

ESTIMATING THE FABRIC QUANTITY

Measure your window to find the finished width and length of the curtains – see 'Measuring up for curtains and blinds' in the Technique know-how section, page 57). To find the depth of your front overhang, divide the length measurement into three and add the new figure to the length. To the new total length measurement, add 26cm (10¼in) for the top and bottom hems, and 6cm (2⅜in) to the width for side hems.

TO MAKE

1 Cut out the required number of fabric drops for your window. Join fabric widths if necessary to obtain the correct width, with flat fell seams (see the Technique know-how section, on page 61).

2 Press a double-turned 1.5cm (⅝in) hem along the side edges and machine stitch in place. Press a double-turned 6cm (2½in) hem along the top and base of the curtain and machine stitch in place. Slipstitch (see Technique know-how, page 63) together the open side edges of the top and base hems.

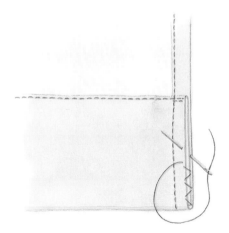

3 Work out the positions of the beads for the top hem. Space them evenly approximately 5cm (2in) apart. Thread a needle with a length of doubled thread and fasten it into the hem at one of the

positions with a couple of stitches. Thread on a round bead, then a leaf bead and finally the bugle bead. Take thread around the last bead and thread the needle back up through the leaf and round bead. Secure thread into the hem with a couple of stitches. Repeat at each position marked to attach the remaining beads.

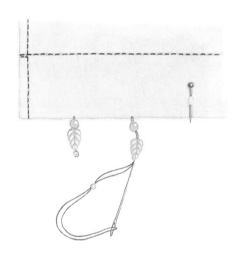

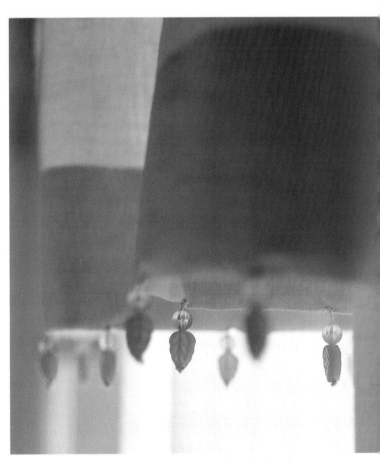

Left: Nothing could be simpler than these long pastel panels draped loosely over a metal pole, they make the perfect curtains for an attractive rustic bedroom. **Above:** The edges of the curtains are decorated with delicate beads stitched at regular intervals along the top hems.

Lavender sachets

MATERIALS

- 20cm (8in) of 114cm- (45in-) wide Ombre Stripe (OS 05); Lilac (SC 36) and Lavender (SC 14) Shot Cottons
- 1.1m (1¼yds) of 10mm- (⅜in-) wide lilac velvet ribbon
- Matching thread
- Dried lavender for filling

TO MAKE

1 From the striped fabric cut two squares 12.5 x 12.5cm (5 x 5in). With right sides facing, raw edges level and using a 1cm (⅜in) seam allowance, machine stitch the two squares together around all sides leaving an opening for turning through.

2 Clip corners and turn each square through to the right side, carefully pushing out the corners. Press seamed edges flat, and then fill the sachet through the opening with lavender. Slipstitch (see Technique know-how, page 63) the opening edges together. Repeat steps 1 and 2 with the remaining two fabrics.

3 When you have completed the three sachets, stack them in a pile and tie them together using the ribbon in the same manner that you would tie up a parcel. Finish ends in a bow and trim away any excess ribbon by cutting off at an angle.

Simple lavender sachets fit neatly into drawers or under your pillows. Tie three together with ribbon as a scented gift for a friend

Stripy cushion

MATERIALS

- 1.10m (1¼yd) of 114cm- (45in-) wide Exotic Stripe (ES 04)
- Matching thread
- 45 x 45cm (18 x 18in) cushion pad

TO MAKE

1 Trace over the Stripy cushion template on page 75. Place fold edge of template to the fold of a piece of paper, trace around the shape and cut out double thickness to complete the template. Using the completed template, cut four triangular pieces. To ensure the design matches up correctly, it is important to lay the long edge of the template along the same coloured stripe every time. From the remaining fabric cut: one small back 31 x 48cm (12 x 19in), and one larger back 34 x 48cm (13½ x 19in), with the stripes running down the longer edges.

2 With right sides facing and stripes matching, baste and machine stitch two of the triangles together along one shorter edge to form one larger triangle. Press the seam open and repeat stitching with remaining two smaller triangles.

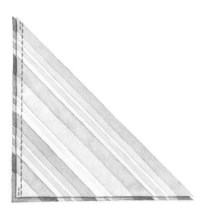

3 With right sides facing and stripes and seams matching, baste and machine stitch the two larger triangles together along the long edges to form a square. Press seams open. Trim away seam turnings at each corner, level with the cushion edges. Turn to the Technique know-how section on page 62, to complete the cushion cover.

This clever patchwork cushion is made from four large striped triangles, which are stitched together to form an interesting kaleidoscopic square

Ruffled cushion

MATERIALS
- 50cm (⅝yd) of 114cm- (45in-) wide Lavender Shot Cotton (SC 14)
- 30cm, or 40cm (12in, or 16in) of 114cm- (45in-) wide Rowan Stripe (RS 05), depending on the width of your ruffle (see step 1)
- Matching thread
- 45 x 45cm (18 x 18in) cushion pad

TO MAKE

1   From the plain fabric cut one front cushion 48 x 48cm (19 x 19in), one small back 31 x 48cm (12 x 19in), and one larger back 34 x 48cm (13½ x 19in). If you have an overlocking machine, cut four strips across the width of the striped fabric 6cm (2⅜in) deep. If you don't own an overlocking machine, you will have to neaten the frill edges with a narrow machine rolled hem, and therefore the strips will need to be cut 7.5cm (3in) wide. Trim off the selvedges from the ends of each strip.

2   Turn to the Technique know-how section on page 62, to complete the main cushion cover, but do not insert the pad.

3   Stitch the striped ruffle strips together to form a ring using French seams (see Technique know-how, page 60). Neaten the circular raw edges with an overlock machine, by working either a rolled hem, or a small closely-worked overlock stitch. Alternatively, if you don't own an overlock machine, turn and machine stitch a double-turned 3mm (⅛in) hem to the wrong side, around each circular edge.

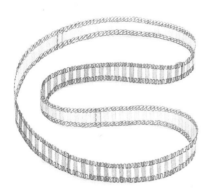

4   Press the circular ruffle in half with wrong sides facing, by bringing the neatened hem edges together. Open out the ruffle and using the pressline as a guide, work a separate row of machine gathering stitches along each of the four strips of fabric that form the ruffle.

5   Carefully pull up the gathers evenly along the ruffle, so that each section fits a side of the cushion cover. Fold the ruffle back in half along the gathered line and pin the gathered edge to the cushion, right along the edge. Invisibly hand-catch the ruffle to the edge of the cushion with small hand-worked stitches. Insert cushion pad through the back opening.

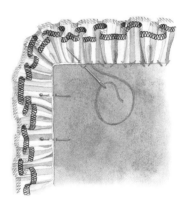

Tassled cushion

MATERIALS
- 50cm (⅝yd) of 114cm- (45in-) wide Gazania (GP 03-S)
- 20cm (8in) of 114cm- (45in-) wide Smoky Shot Cotton (SC 20)
- 20cm (8in) of 114cm- (45in-) wide Lavender Shot Cotton (SC 14)
- Four 25mm (1in) diameter wooden beads
- Matching thread
- 45 x 45cm (18 x 18in) cushion pad

TO MAKE

1   From the print fabric cut: one front cushion 48 x 48cm (19 x 19in), one small back 31 x 48cm (12 x 19in), and one larger back 34 x 48cm (13½ x 19in). From each of the plain coloured fabrics cut four squares 16 x 16cm (6¼ x 6¼in).

2   Turn to the Technique know-how section on page 62 to complete the main cushion cover, but do not insert the pad.

3   Place the Lavender squares on top of the Smoky squares, with raw edges level and right sides facing. Taking a 1cm (⅜in) seam allowance, stitch the squares together around all edges, leaving an opening along one side. Clip corners and turn each square through to the right side, carefully pushing out the corners. Press flat and slipstitch (see Technique know-how, page 63) the opening edges together.

4 To form a tassel, place a wooden bead in the centre of a square with the Lavender side uppermost, and gather the fabric up around it with the fingers. Using a needle and doubled thread, make a small stitch in the Smoky fabric at the top of the bead to secure. Then, wind the thread around the outside of the gathered square several times to hold the bead in place. Fasten off the thread with a stitch as before. Repeat this step with remaining squares.

5 Using a needle and doubled thread make a stitch at one corner point of the main cushion cover to secure the thread. Then, securely stitch the bead end of a tassel to the point of the cushion cover. Repeat stitching at the remaining corners of the cushion. Insert cushion pad through the back opening.

Add style to basic cushion covers with stripy, ruffled edgings, or hand-made tassels

BATHROOM

For a serene bathroom to refresh your spirit, choose rebalancing fabrics in greys, black and neutrals. Combine all three in the softest rag bathmat and toning laundry bag, adding a touch of vitality with an easy kimono-style robe and edged flannels in a striking monochrome pattern

Bring calm to your bathroom with
this stylish Zen shower curtain,
which simply hangs in front of
your existing shower curtain

Zen shower curtain

MATERIALS

- 4.10m (4½yds) of 114cm- (45in-) wide Shot Cotton in Ecru (SC 24)
- 20cm (8in) of 114cm- (45in-) wide Shot Cotton in Stone Grey (SC 23)
- 20cm (8in) of 114cm- (45in-) wide Shot Cotton in Charcoal (SC 25)
- Matching thread
- Twelve 11mm (⅜in) silver eyelets
- 15cm (6in) of 90cm-(35½in-) wide lightweight iron-on interfacing
- Two skeins of stone coloured stranded embroidery thread
- Embroidery hoop
- Tear-away backing
- Dressmakers' carbon paper
- A white nylon shower curtain, approximately 178 x 178cm (70 x 70in)

TO MAKE

1 From the main Ecru coloured fabric, cut two panels 96 x 200cm (37¾ x 78¾in). From the interfacing, cut three strips, 3 x 90cm (1¼ x 35½in). From one of the interfacing strips cut two short lengths 7.5cm (3in) long.

2 With glue side down, lay one long and one short interfacing strip on the wrong side of each fabric panel, along one short edge, overlapping the ends of the interfacing. Using a hot iron and a pressing cloth, press the interfacing in place. Repeat with remaining panel and interfacing pieces.

3 With right sides facing and making sure the two interfaced ends are level, join the two fabric panels together along one long edge with a French seam (see the Technique know-how section, page 60), to form the full curtain. Press the seam to one side.

4 Press a double-turned 1.2cm (½in) hem to the wrong side, along the side edges of the joined fabric panels, and machine stitch in place. Press a double-turned 5cm (2in) hem to the wrong side, along the base edge (not interfaced), and machine stitch in place. Finally, press a double-turned 3cm (1¼in) hem to the wrong side, along the top interfaced edge, and machine stitch in place. Slipstitch (see Technique know-how, page 63) together the open side edges of the top and base hems.

5 Cut both the Charcoal and Stone Grey fabric strips into four-equal sized pieces. Using the dressmakers' carbon paper, transfer the outline of an Oriental character (see page 78) on to the centre of each piece. Hoop one of the fabric pieces in the embroidery frame, placing the motif in the centre, and with a piece of tear-away backing underneath.

6 Using two strands of stranded embroidery thread, work over the design with satin stitch (see Technique know-how, page 63), until the motif is completely filled. Remove fabric from frame and tear away the remaining backing. Carefully press flat. Using the template on page 78, and placing the embroidered motif centrally, cut out an appliqué patch. Embroider remaining fabric pieces in the same way and cut out the individual patches.

7 Press a 1cm (⅜in) hem to the wrong side round each embroidered patch. Lay out the curtain right side up on a large flat surface. Arrange the patches in two rows down each side edge of the curtain, alternating the colours and placing them 6.5cm (2½in) in from the edge, 20cm (8in) from the top and the rest spaced approximately 26.5cm (10½in) apart. Pin, and baste them in place. Using six strands of the embroidery thread, appliqué the patches in place with a small running stitch (see Technique know-how, page 63), worked 3mm (⅛in) in from the edge. Remove all basting stitches.

8 Mark the eyelet positions centrally along the top interfaced hem of the curtain, using a pencil. Place the first and last eyelet 3.5cm (1⅜in) in from each side edge, and space the remaining eyelets 16cm (6¼in) apart. Insert eyelets following the manufacturer's instructions. Place the nylon shower curtain behind your new curtain, line up the eyelets and hang both layers together, by threading the shower curtain rings through both sets of eyelets.

NOTE: When taking a shower ensure that your fabric curtain is hanging outside the bath or shower tray to stop it getting wet, whilst the nylon one should hang inside.

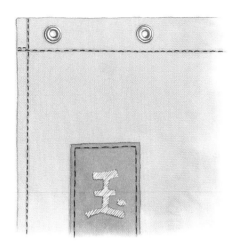

The contrasting patches are decorated with embroidered characters, and appliquéd to the curtain using hand-worked running stitches

Laundry bags

MATERIALS FOR ONE BAG

■ 80cm (1yd) of 114cm- (45in-) wide Shot Cotton in either Ecru (SC 24), Stone Grey (SC 23) or Charcoal (SC 25)
■ 80cm (1yd) of 114cm- (45in-) wide calico
■ Matching thread
■ 1.3m (1½yds) of No 6 piping cord, in cream

TO MAKE

1 From both the Shot Cotton and calico cut out a panel 73 x 111cm (28¾ x 43¾in). With right sides facing, stitch the two panels together along one long edge, with a 1.5cm (⅝in) seam allowance. Press the seam open.

2 With right sides facing, fold the joined panels in half, with the seam running horizontally, so seam ends meet. Pin and baste all edges together. Mark

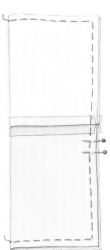

with a pin the position of the top of the draw cord opening on shot cotton part of bag, by measuring 4.5cm (1¾in) down from the central seam. For the bottom of the opening, measure down a further 3cm (1¼in) and mark with a second pin.

3 Machine stitch the bag together around all three sides with a 1.5cm (⅝in) seam allowance, leaving an opening between the pins for the draw cord (make sure you reverse stitch at each side of the opening to secure), and another larger opening along the top edge of the calico for turning through. Turn bag through to right side and push out the corners well on the Shot Cotton part of the bag. Machine, or hand stitch the opening in the calico fabric closed, and lightly press the bag.

These handy bags will keep your laundry neatly out of the way. Make one for each member of the family, or colour code them to help sort out the washing

4 Push the calico lining down inside the bag, and roll the top seam between your fingers and thumbs to ensure it lies right along the edge. Press top seamed edge flat. Baste around top edge. To form the draw cord channel, work two rows of machine stitches round the top of the bag, one 4.5cm (1¾in), and the other 7.5cm (3in) down from the top edge. Remove basting stitches and thread the cord through the channel and back out. Knot ends together to secure.

Rag bath mat

Approximate finished size: 48 x 84cm (19 x 33in)

MATERIALS
- 2.8m (3¼yds) of 114cm- (45in-) wide Shot Cotton in Ecru (SC 24)
- 2.6m (3yds) of 114cm- (45in-) wide Shot Cotton in Stone Grey (SC 23) and Charcoal (SC 25)
- 2.6m (3yds) of 114cm- (45in-) wide Stone Damask (GP 02-S)
- 63 x 99cm (24¾ x 39in) of hessian
- Pinking shears
- Tapestry frame or large picture frame, measuring same size as the hessian
- Marker pen
- Ruler
- Rug hook
- Strong adhesive fabric glue

Note: The following instructions are written for a right-handed person. Simply reverse the directions if you are left-handed.

TO MAKE

1 Stretch the hessian on to the frame. Using the ruler and marker pen, draw a border round the hessian, on the right side, placed 7.5cm (3in) in from the edge. Then, draw approximately 65 vertical lines down the hessian, inside the border, spaced 1.2cm (½in) apart, to mark the striped design.

2 Using the pinking shears, cut up all the different fabrics into strips across the width, each approximately 4cm (1⅝in) deep.

3 Start working with the right side of the hessian facing upwards, and holding the hook in your right hand and an Ecru rag strip underneath the frame in your left hand. Working from right to left, push the hook through the hessian to make a hole, at the end of the first line, and pick up the strip. Bring the end of the strip up to the right side. Push the hook back down through the hessian approximately 6mm (¼in) to the left, along the line, and pick up a loop of strip. Bring through to the right side and leave a loop about 1.5cm (⅝in) on top of the hessian. Continue until the fabric strip is used up.

4 Finish the strip by bringing the end through to the right side. Start the next strip in the same hole as the last end. Continue in the same colour until you reach the end of the line. Complete the rug working alternate coloured lines. When the rug is complete, remove the hessian from the frame and press with a hot iron over a damp cloth on both sides. Turn the hessian border under and glue in place.

Step out of your bath on to this luxurious cotton bath mat.
It's deceptively easy to make out of strips of fabric

Floral Kimono

MATERIALS
- 3.4m (3⅔yds) of 114cm- (45in-) wide Stone Damask (GP 02-S)
- Matching thread
- Large piece of paper

TO MAKE

1 Scale up the kimono pattern pieces on to a large piece of paper, as indicated on pages 76 and 77. Using full-sized pattern pieces cut two fronts, one back, two sleeves, two pockets, two front & back neck bands, three back neck & belt loop strips and one belt.

2 Neaten the top edge of each pocket and press 4cm (1½in) to the wrong side. Machine stitch in place 3.5cm (1⅜in) from the pressed edge. Press remaining edges of pockets 1.5cm (⅝in) to the wrong side, and baste them in place.

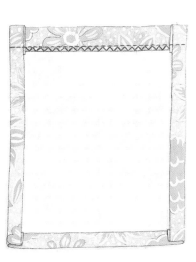

3 Place a pocket centrally on to the right side of one front, with the base edge 26cm (10¼in) up from the hem edge. Pin, baste and machine stitch in place close to the pressed edges. Reverse stitch at the top edges to secure. Repeat with remaining pocket and front.

4 Stitch fronts to back at the shoulder seams, with a 1.5cm (⅝in) seam allowance. Neaten seam turnings together and press them towards the back. Topstitch turnings in place working 6mm (¼in) away from the seamline.

5 To make the back neck loop, press the long raw edges over to the wrong side to meet at the centre. Fold the strip in half along its length by bringing the long pressed edges together to enclose the raw edges. Press flat. Machine stitch loop edges together down the side edge. Repeat for the belt loops.

6 Pin and baste the short raw ends of the back neck loop to the wrong side of the centre back neck, keeping raw edges level. Repeat with the belt loops placing one on the right side of each front, at the side edges, 53cm (21in) up from the hem edge.

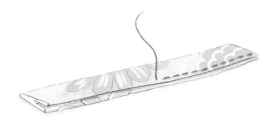

Left: This lightweight kimono bathrobe, with a tie belt and patch pockets, is easy to make and even easier to wear

7 With right sides facing, stitch a sleeve into each armhole, with a 1.5cm (⅝in) seam allowance. Neaten turnings together and press towards the body. Topstitch turnings in place working 6mm (¼in) away from the seamline.

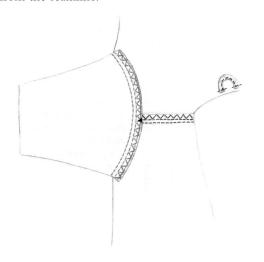

8 With right sides facing, stitch fronts to back at side seams and underarms, in one continuous line of stitching; matching hem edges, underarm seams, and sandwiching the belt loops in place at the same time.

9 Stitch the two front and back neck bands together at one short end, with right sides facing and taking a 1cm (⅜in) seam allowance. Press seam open. Fold band in half along its length, by bringing the long raw edges together, enclosing the seam turnings. Press band flat and baste the long raw edges together.

10 Matching the central seam of the band to the centre back neck, pin and baste the band to the front

and back neck edges, right sides together, with a 1cm (⅜in) seam allowance. Machine stitch in place sandwiching the back neck loop in place at the same time. Neaten turnings together and press towards the body. Topstitch turnings in place, working 6mm (¼in) away from the seamline.

11 Neaten the sleeve and body hem edges, press 3cm (1¼in) to the wrong side and machine stitch in place.

12 With right sides facing, fold belt in half along its length, and machine stitch together along the long edges and across one short end with a 1cm (⅜in) seam allowance. Clip corners and turn through to right side. Fold raw edges at the open end 1cm (⅜in) to wrong side, and slipstitch (see Technique know-how, page 63) together. Press belt flat and topstitch 6mm (¼in) in from the edge around all sides.

Edged face cloths

MATERIALS FOR ONE FACE CLOTH

■ A white terry towelling face cloth
■ 135cm (53in) of 2.5cm- (1in-) wide bias binding in Stone Damask (GP 02-S), see 'Making bias binding' in the Technique know-how, on page 61
■ Matching thread

TO MAKE

1 When you purchase your face cloth, you may find that the edges are simply overlocked with rounded corners – if this is the case, you do not need to do anything to them. But, if your face cloth is square with machined hems, you will need to trim them away and round off the corners before you can edge them with fabric.

2 To finish the edges of your face cloth with fabric, press the length of bias binding in half along its length with the turnings inside. Place the binding over the edge of the face cloth, and pin and baste in place. For a neat finish to the ends of the bias binding, press them 1cm (⅜in) to the wrong side and butt them up close together. Machine stitch the binding in place close to the inner edges of the binding. Remove all basting stitches.

Give your face cloths a designer makeover with some pretty floral edgings

TECHNIQUE KNOW-HOW

Home sewing is like any other skill – once you have the basic techniques and know-how it's much easier to get successful results. In this chapter you'll find some basic techniques and easy tricks of the trade to help you achieve a more professional finish to your projects. Plus a straightforward glossary to demystify the jargon and help you on your way.

Measuring up for curtains and blinds

It's best to have all your tracks and fittings in place before you begin to measure, including carpets for full length curtains.

For accuracy use a long, retractable steel tape measure and ask someone to help you when measuring larger windows.

Take your time when measuring up. It's important to get the measuring correct to avoid expensive mistakes when buying and cutting out your fabric. Take your finished length measurement a few times across the window, as floors can be uneven, and check whether your window is true by measuring the width at both the top and the bottom. Check every measurement twice, but don't worry unduly, as small measuring mistakes can usually be rectified.

Curtains

MEASURING FOR CURTAINS

There are two basic measurements you need to find out before estimating how much fabric you're going to need:

- The length of the curtain from the track or pole to the floor (measurement B) or windowsill (measurement C), depending on what you have in mind.

- The length of the curtain track or pole (measurement A), plus any overlap arms at the centre if your track has them.

CURTAIN LENGTH

- For curtains hung from an exposed track, you'll need to work out where your heading tape will finish in relation to your track. If you're not sure, hook a piece of the heading tape on to your track and measure down from the top of your tape.

- For curtains hung from a pole, measure the length from the base of the curtain ring.

- For curtains hung from a track screwed to a pelmet board, measure the finished length from the underside of the board. Then, work out the hook drop. This will depend on the type of heading tape and curtain track you are using. If you're not sure, hook a piece of the chosen tape on to the track and measure the clearance between the top edge of the tape and the base of the board.

- For full-length curtains, deduct 1cm (⅜in) from measurement B (see diagram below) for clearance. If you want to make your curtains drape on the floor, add 5-20cm (2-8in) to measurement B.

- For sill-length curtains, if your windowsill protrudes out a long way, deduct 1cm (⅜in) from measurement C (see diagram below); this will allow the curtains to hang clear. If possible try to make curtains hang just below the sill, as this looks more attractive. To do this, add 5-10cm (2-4in) to measurement C.

Before you can work out your fabric quantity, you will need to decide whether your curtain is to be gathered at the top. If this is the case, you will usually require a heading tape. Heading tapes contain pockets for inserting hooks and have draw cords running through them. After the tape is attached to the curtain, the cords are pulled up to gather the fabric to your finished curtain width.

- Standard heading tape is 2.5cm (1in) deep and needs a fabric fullness of 1½ to 2 times the length of your track or pole. It has one row of pockets and is usually applied 3cm (1¼in) from the top edge of the curtain.

- Pencil pleat heading tape is 7.5cm (3in) deep and needs a fabric fullness of 2½ - 3 times the length of your track or pole. It has two or three rows of pockets and is applied close to the top edge of your curtain.

Blinds

Blinds can be fixed either inside or outside the window recess. Inside (recess-fixed) is neater for pull-up or Roman blinds, but will block out some daylight and can obstruct the window from opening. Blinds hung outside (face-fixed) give more flexibility as regards size and can make a window appear larger.

POSITIONING BLIND SUPPORTS

- A recess-fixed blind is held in place with a timber support (see opposite) screwed to the top of the window recess (measurement E).

- For a face-fixed blind, the timber support is screwed to the wall with brackets (see opposite page). The support should be positioned 12.5cm (5in) above the window and with the same distance each side of the window(measurement F).

MEASURING FOR BLINDS

- For the finished length of a recess-fixed blind, measure from the top of the timber support (measurement G; see diagram right). The finished width is the width of the recess (measurement E) minus 2cm (¾in), so the blind does not touch the sides of the window, which could restrict it from moving up and down.

- For the finished length of a face-fixed blind, measure from the top of the timber support down to 5cm (2in) below the window-sill (measurement H). However, if your sill projects out a long way, subtract 1cm (⅜in) from the length for the blind to hang just clear of it. The finished width is the length of the timber support (measurement F) plus 1.5cm (⅝in).

Making and fixing a timber support

The support should be made from 2.5 x 5cm (1 x 2in) timber covered in fabric, to match the blind, or painted to match the wall or window frame.

1 Cut the support to the finished width of the blind less 1.5cm (⅝in) for a face-fixed blind, and 3cm (1¼in) less than the width of the window recess for a recessed blind. With recessed blinds the support is usually fixed directly to the roof of the recess itself.

2 For a recess-fixed blind only, drill two holes 15cm (6in) in from each end on the wide side of the timber. For both the recess and face-fixed blinds, cover the timber with fabric and staple or glue in place, or paint the timber to match your decor.

3 Staple the hook side of a length of touch-and-close tape to one of the long narrow sides of the timber support. For a face-fixed blind without a pelmet over the top, you can fix the hook side of the touch-and-close tape on top of the timber support (ie. one of the wider sides). This will hide your machine stitching at the top of the blind from view, but remember to allow the extra length at the top when measuring for your blind length.

4 Using a bradawl, mark the positions of the screw eyes on the wide underside of the timber support. Line them up with the rows of cording rings on your blind and screw them in place. Screw an extra eye 2cm (¾in) in from one end of the support, at the cord operating end.

5 For a recess-fixed blind, pierce the fabric covering your drilled holes and screw the support to the roof of the recess.

6 For a face-fixed blind, screw small angle brackets to the underside of each end of the support. Drill fixing holes in the wall and screw the brackets in place, approximately 12.5cm (5in) above the window.

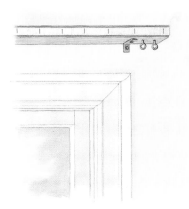

How much fabric do I need?

■ First, calculate how many fabric widths are needed: for blinds and flat curtains, add your hem allowances to the width measurement and divide this number by the width of your fabric. For curtains with fullness, multiply the length of the track or pole by the fullness required (see Curtain fullness and heading tapes, on the opposite page) and divide this number by the width of your fabric. Round up to the nearest fabric width.

■ Next, calculate the total quantity required; add the top and base hem allowances to the length measurement (see individual projects) and multiply this number by the amount of fabric widths you've just calculated.

■ If your fabric has a pattern repeat, add one full design repeat per fabric width after the first width.

How much heading tape do I need?

Multiply the number of fabric widths required by the width of your fabric, then add 20cm.

Stitching Basics

Plain straight seams

This is the most commonly used seam for joining fabric widths together in curtain making. It is best to take a 2cm (¾in) seam allowance unless otherwise stated.

1 With right sides together, machine stitch along the seamline, reverse stitching for a few stitches at both ends of the seam to secure the threads.

2 For speed and to avoid basting seams prior to machine stitching, pin seams at right angles to the seamline and then machine slowly over the pins, taking care not to hit one, as it could break the needle.

3 Using a steam iron, press the seam open flat.

FRENCH SEAMS

This is a self-neatening seam, used mainly on sheer and lightweight fabrics.

1 With wrong sides facing, pin and then baste the two edges together especially if the fabric is slippery. Machine stitch seam together 6mm (¼in) in from the raw edges and trim turnings to 3mm (⅛in), as shown.

2 Press the seam open and then refold with right sides together and stitchline placed exactly on the folded edge. Press again and pin, then stitch 1cm (⅜in) in from the seamed edge, enclosing the raw edges. Press finished seam to one side.

FLAT FELL SEAMS

This is another self-neatening seam, which is stronger and flatter than a French seam.

1 With right sides together, stitch a plain straight seam. Press both seam allowances to one side and then trim the lower seam allowance to 6mm (¼in).

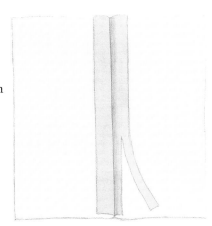

2 Fold the edge of the top seam allowance under to enclose the trimmed raw edge. Press this fold flat. Pin at right angles to the seam and stitch it to the main fabric close to the pressed edge.

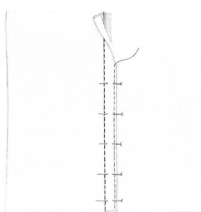

Making bias binding

1 Bias binding is cut on the cross, which means it's cut at an angle to the warp and weft threads of the fabric. To find the bias of the fabric, fold the raw edge (running across the width of the fabric from selvedge to selvedge) down to form a triangle so that it lies parallel to one of the selvedges. Press and cut along the line.

2 Draw pencil lines parallel to the bias, to the required width. This should be twice the finished flat width of the binding required. Cut along these lines, until you have the required number of strips to form the length of binding to go round the edge of your project.

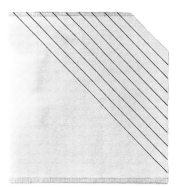

3 To join the strips together, the two ends that are to be joined must be cut at a 45 degree angle, as shown in diagram A. Stitch the pieces together with right sides facing, trim the seam turnings and press the seams open – see diagram B.

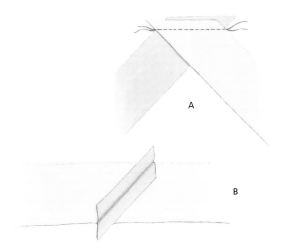

4 With wrong sides facing, press the strip in half along its length. Then open the strip out flat and press the long raw edges over to the wrong side to meet at the central pressline.

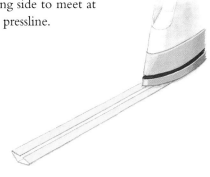

MITRED CORNERS

Mitres form neat flat corners, which are particularly useful for bulky fabrics.

1 Press over the required hem allowances along each side. Open out the deeper hems, then using the inner finished corner point as a pivot and matching up the press lines, fold over a triangular corner.

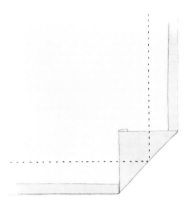

2 Trim away the excess fabric from the folded over corner, to leave a 1.5cm (5/8in) seam allowance.

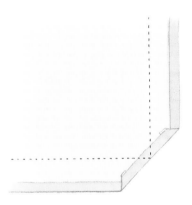

3 Refold the hems to form the mitre and slipstitch the pressed diagonal edges together.

Completing the cushions

1 Press a double-turned 1.5cm (⅝in) hem to the wrong side down one long edge of each back cushion piece, and machine stitch in place close to the first pressed edge.

2 Lay the cushion front face up on a flat surface and place the larger cushion back face down on top of the front, with raw edges level. Place the smaller back face down on top of the uncovered side of the front cushion cover, keeping raw edges level and overlapping the hemmed edges.

3 Baste the cushion cover pieces together round all sides. Machine stitch round all four edges with a 1.5cm (⅝in) seam allowance. Neaten turnings together, remove basting stitches, clip corners and turn cover through to right side.

Useful stitches

Note: The following stitches are worked for a right-handed person. Simply reverse them if you are left-handed.

BASTING STITCH

This is a temporary stitch used to hold two pieces of fabric together. Make long stitches just inside the stitchline, until you're ready to stitch permanently. Use a bright coloured thread so that it's easy to see when removing.

SLIPSTITCH

This stitch is used to join two folded edges together. Working from right to left, bring the needle out through one folded edge. Slip the needle through the fold of the opposite edge for about 6mm (¼in) and draw the needle and thread through. Continue in this manner until pieces are joined.

SLIP HEMMING

This stitch is used to hold a folded edge to a flat surface. It is almost invisible on the right side and is worked from right to left with the needle almost parallel to the stitching line.

Bring the needle out of the fold of the fabric and pick up two threads from the fabric directly below. Take the needle back into the folded edge and run the needle inside the fold for approximately 1cm (⅜in). Bring the needle out and draw the thread through. Continue in the same manner, making sure the stitches are not pulled too tightly, or the fabric will look puckered on the right side.

RUNNING STITCH

A short, even stitch for seaming or gathering. Worked like basting, except the stitches are smaller and permanent. Keep the stitches and spaces even in size for the best effect.

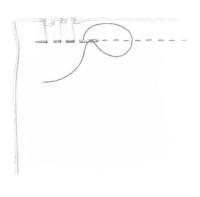

OVERCAST STITCH

This is the customary hand stitch for finishing raw edges of fabric to prevent them from fraying. In general, the more the fabric frays, the deeper and closer together the stitches should be worked. Working from either direction, take diagonal stitches over the edge, spacing them an even distance apart at a uniform depth.

SATIN STITCH

This is a freestyle embroidery stitch, which is worked over a design that has been traced, printed or transferred on to a fabric.

Work straight stitches closely together across the shape on your design, as shown in the diagram below. The most important thing is to try to keep a good shape to your edge, and don't make the stitches too long, otherwise they are liable to catch on things and pull out of position.

Glossary of terms

Appliqué The technique of stitching fabric shapes on to a background to create a design. It can be applied either by hand or machine with a decorative embroidery stitch, such as buttonhole or satin stitch.

Basting Also known as tacking in Great Britain. This is a means of holding fabric layers together temporarily with large hand stitches.

Bias The diagonal *grain* of a fabric. This is the direction which has the most give or stretch, making it ideal for bindings, especially when used on curved edges.

Binding A strip of fabric, either straight-grain or bias (cut on the diagonal). Can be used to bind edges, or for piping.

Bradawl This is a pointed tool with a handle used for making holes in timber.

Bump A soft, blanket-like fabric used as interlining.

Calico A raw unbleached cotton with a plain weave.

Chalk pencils Available in various colours, they are used for marking lines or spots on fabric. Some pencils have a brush attached, although marks are easily removed.

Cleat A double-pronged hook which secures the cords of blinds.

Dressmakers' carbon paper Sometimes sold as tracing paper. Available in a number of colours, for light or dark fabric. It can be used with pencils, or a tracing wheel to transfer a design on to fabric.

Embroidery hoop Consists of two wooden circular or oval rings with a screw adjuster on the outer ring. It stabilises the fabric, helping to create an even tension for stitching.

Eyelet A two-part metal ring which can be inserted into the heading of curtains or blinds, to hang them from a pole.

Face-fixed Fixing blinds and curtains outside the window recess.

Fade away marker pen A special felt tip pen for making marks on the right side of fabric as a guide for stitching. The marks gradually fade away without the use of water.

Finished drop The length of the finished curtain when hung.

Finished width The measurement from side edge to side edge once the curtain is gathered up.

Flat fell seams See the Technique know-how section, page 61.

French seams See the Technique know-how section, page 60.

Grain The direction in which the threads run in a woven fabric. In a vertical direction it is called the lengthwise grain, which has very little stretch. The horizontal direction, or crosswise grain is slightly stretchy, but diagonally the fabric has a lot of stretch. The diagonal grain is called the *bias*.

Hessian Coarse, heavyweight fabric made from jute, hemp or cotton.

Iron-on interfacing eg. Vilene/Pellon. A non-woven supporting material with adhesive that melts when ironed, making the interfacing adhere to the fabric.

Leading edge The side edge of the curtain that will be at the centre when the curtains are closed. Or, on a single curtain, the edge that you draw across.

Mitring See the Technique know-how section, page 62.

Overcast stitch See the Technique know-how section, page 63.

Overlock machine (or serger) This machine does not replace a conventional sewing machine, but compliments it. Overlocking is a quick way of finishing off seams and hem edges, as it cuts and neatens in one operation.

Paper-backed adhesive web eg. Bondaweb/Wonder-Under. Can be cut to shape and pressed to the wrong side of a fabric shape using a hot iron. Then the paper backing is peeled off. The fabric shape can then be placed on top of another, adhesive side down, and pressed again to fuse in place.

Patchwork The technique of stitching small pieces of fabric together to create a larger piece of fabric, usually forming a design.

Pelmet board A horizontal board used to support a pelmet above curtains or a blind.

Pencil pleat heading A curtain heading formed with a tape which creates a row of densely-packed narrow pleats.

Pinking shears These cut with a zigzag fray-resistant edge. Excellent for finishing seams and raw edges on many types of fabric; also for creating decorative edges.

Pins Use good quality pins. Do not use thick, burred or rusted pins which will leave holes or marks. Long pins with glass or plastic heads are easier to use when pinning through thick fabrics.

Quilting Traditionally done by hand with running stitches, but for speed a machine is usually used. The stitches are sewn through the top, *padding* and *backing* to hold the three layers together. Quilting stitches are usually worked in some form of design, but they can be random.

Recessed window A window set back into a wall. You can hang a blind or curtain inside it.

Satin stitch See the Technique know-how section, page 63.

Seam allowance The narrow strip of raw-edged fabric left after making a seam, to allow for fraying.

Selvedges Also known as selvages, these are the firmly-woven edges down each side of a fabric length. Selvedges should be trimmed off before cutting out your fabric, as they are more liable to shrink when the fabric is washed.

Slip hemming See the Technique know-how section, page 63.

Slipstitch See the Technique know-how section, page 63.

Tailor's chalk These are wedge-shaped pieces of chalk, available in several colours for marking on positions to your fabric.

Tapestry frame This is used to keep fabric taut while you're working on it. The frame usually has two horizontal rollers, each with a piece of tape attached along its length. The side rails can be straight or come with a screw thread, which allows the horizontal rollers to be adjusted.

Tear-away backing A non-woven material resembling parchment placed underneath fabric to support it while embroidering by machine or hand.

Touch-and-close fastener eg. Velcro. Composed of two tape strips, one with a looped nap and the other with a hooked nap. When pressed together, the surfaces grip and remain locked until they are pulled apart.

Track Metal or plastic runners from which a curtain is hung.

Warp These are the yarns running along the length of a fabric, parallel to the selvedges. They are usually stronger, and sometimes thicker than the weft threads running at right angles to them.

Weft These are the yarns running across the width of the fabric and interlocking with the warp yarns.

Abbreviations
The Kaffe Fassett Fabric collection

Stripes

NS	Narrow Stripe
PS	Pachrangi Stripe
ES	Exotic Stripe
AS	Alternate Stripe
BS	Broad Stripe
OS	Ombre Stripe
BWS	Blue and White Stripe
RS	Rowan Stripe

Checks

NC	Narrow Check
BC	Broad Check
EC	Exotic Check

Prints

GP 01	Roman Glass
GP 02	Damask
GP 03	Gazania
GP 07	Artichokes
GP 08	Forget-me-not Rose
GP 09	Chard
GP 11	Flower Lattice
GP 12	Floral Dance
GP 13	Chrysanthemum
GP 14	Dotty
GP 15	Bubbles
PR	Pressed Roses

Print colour numbers

L	Leafy
J	Jewel
S	Stones
C	Circus
P	Pastel
R	Red
BW	Blue and White
PK	Pink
G	Gold
M	Magenta
O	Ochre
MV	Mauve
GRY	Grey
CT	Citrus
SB	Sky Blue
COB	Colbat
GRN	Green
PL	Plum
B	Blue
SG	Sea Green

TC	Terracotta
D	Driftwood
LV	Lavender
SU	Summer

Shot Cottons

SC 01	Ginger
SC 02	Cassis
SC 03	Prune
SC 04	Slate
SC 05	Opal
SC 06	Thunder
SC 07	Persimmon
SC 08	Raspberry
SC 09	Pomegranate
SC 10	Bittersweet
SC 11	Tangerine
SC 12	Chartreuse
SC 13	Navy
SC 14	Lavender
SC 15	Denim Blue
SC 16	Mustard
SC 17	Sage
SC 18	Tobacco
SC 19	Lichen
SC 20	Smoky
SC 21	Pine
SC 22	Pewter
SC 23	Stone Grey
SC 24	Ecru
SC 25	Charcoal
SC 26	Duck Egg
SC 27	Grass
SC 28	Blush
SC 29	Putty
SC 30	Custard
SC 31	Mushroom
SC 32	Rosy
SC 33	Water Melon
SC 34	Lemon
SC 35	Sunshine
SC 36	Lilac
SC 37	Coffee
SC 38	Biscuit
SC 39	Apple
SC 40	Cobalt
SC 41	Jade
SC 42	Rush
SC 43	Lime

The Kaffe Fassett Fabric Collection

The Kaffe Fassett fabrics are available at Rowan stockists in Europe and the Far East. In USA, Canada and Australia they are available through Westminster stockists and better fabric shops. Please call Rowan Tel: +44 (0) 1484 681881 for stockist details.

100% COTTON ■ **FABRIC WIDTH 114cm (45in)**   Please note: Due to printing, colours may not be true to life.

Shot Cotton

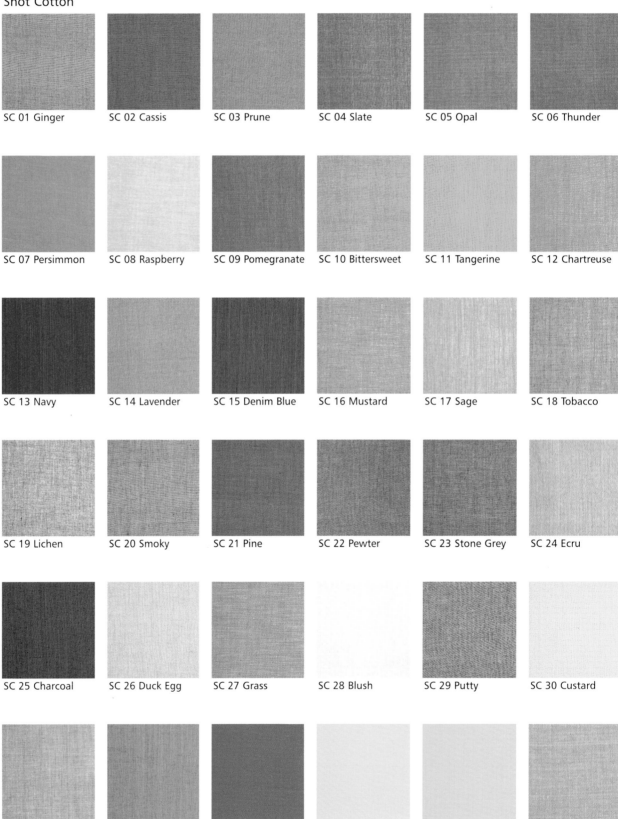

SC 01 Ginger SC 02 Cassis SC 03 Prune SC 04 Slate SC 05 Opal SC 06 Thunder

SC 07 Persimmon SC 08 Raspberry SC 09 Pomegranate SC 10 Bittersweet SC 11 Tangerine SC 12 Chartreuse

SC 13 Navy SC 14 Lavender SC 15 Denim Blue SC 16 Mustard SC 17 Sage SC 18 Tobacco

SC 19 Lichen SC 20 Smoky SC 21 Pine SC 22 Pewter SC 23 Stone Grey SC 24 Ecru

SC 25 Charcoal SC 26 Duck Egg SC 27 Grass SC 28 Blush SC 29 Putty SC 30 Custard

SC 31 Mushroom SC 32 Rosy SC 33 Water Melon SC 34 Lemon SC 35 Sunshine SC 36 Lilac

■ **WASH FABRIC BEFORE USE.**

Prewash all new fabrics before you begin to ensure that there will be no uneven shrinkage and no bleeding of colours in later laundering. Press the fabric whilst it is still damp to return crispness to it.

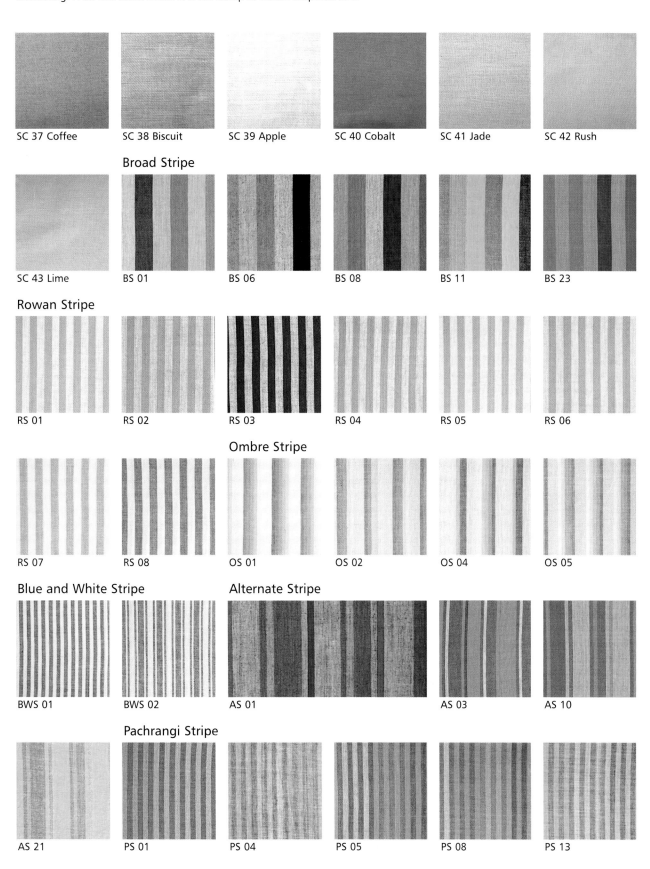

SC 37 Coffee   SC 38 Biscuit   SC 39 Apple   SC 40 Cobalt   SC 41 Jade   SC 42 Rush

Broad Stripe

SC 43 Lime   BS 01   BS 06   BS 08   BS 11   BS 23

Rowan Stripe

RS 01   RS 02   RS 03   RS 04   RS 05   RS 06

Ombre Stripe

RS 07   RS 08   OS 01   OS 02   OS 04   OS 05

Blue and White Stripe   Alternate Stripe

BWS 01   BWS 02   AS 01   AS 03   AS 10

Pachrangi Stripe

AS 21   PS 01   PS 04   PS 05   PS 08   PS 13

Exotic Stripe

PS 15   PS 22   ES 01   ES 04   ES 06

ES 10   ES 15   ES 16   ES 20   ES 21   ES 23

Narrow Stripe

NS 01   NS 08   NS 09   NS 13   NS 16   NS 17

Broad Check

Narrow Check

BC O1   BC 02   BC 03   BC 04   NC 01   NC 02

Exotic Check

NC 03   NC 05   EC 01   EC 02   EC 03   EC 05

Pressed Roses

PR 01   PR 02   PR 03   PR 04   PR 05

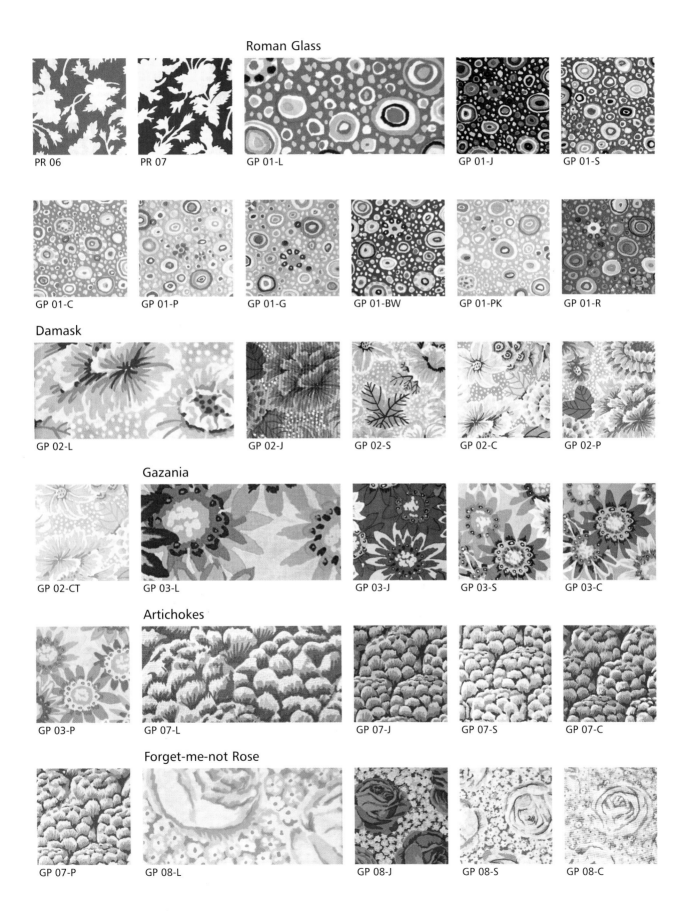

Roman Glass

PR 06   PR 07   GP 01-L   GP 01-J   GP 01-S

GP 01-C   GP 01-P   GP 01-G   GP 01-BW   GP 01-PK   GP 01-R

Damask

GP 02-L   GP 02-J   GP 02-S   GP 02-C   GP 02-P

Gazania

GP 02-CT   GP 03-L   GP 03-J   GP 03-S   GP 03-C

Artichokes

GP 03-P   GP 07-L   GP 07-J   GP 07-S   GP 07-C

Forget-me-not Rose

GP 07-P   GP 08-L   GP 08-J   GP 08-S   GP 08-C

Chard

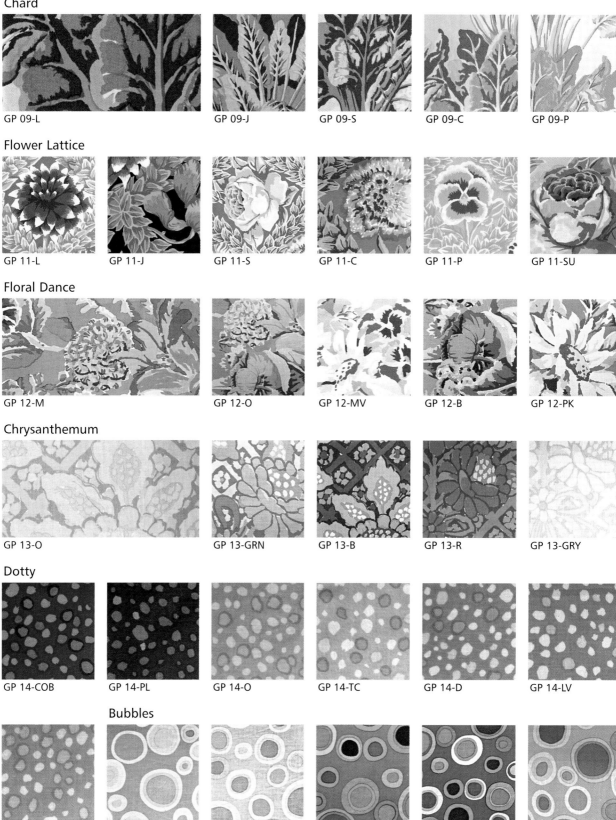

GP 09-L   GP 09-J   GP 09-S   GP 09-C   GP 09-P

Flower Lattice

GP 11-L   GP 11-J   GP 11-S   GP 11-C   GP 11-P   GP 11-SU

Floral Dance

GP 12-M   GP 12-O   GP 12-MV   GP 12-B   GP 12-PK

Chrysanthemum

GP 13-O   GP 13-GRN   GP 13-B   GP 13-R   GP 13-GRY

Dotty

GP 14-COB   GP 14-PL   GP 14-O   GP 14-TC   GP 14-D   GP 14-LV

Bubbles

GP 14-SG   GP 15-O   GP 15-GRY   GP 15-PL   GP 15-COB   GP 15-SB

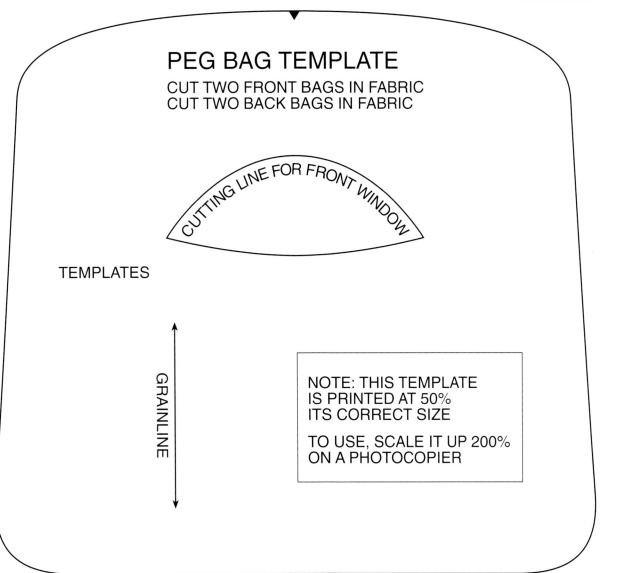

PEG BAG TEMPLATE
CUT TWO FRONT BAGS IN FABRIC
CUT TWO BACK BAGS IN FABRIC

CUTTING LINE FOR FRONT WINDOW

TEMPLATES

GRAINLINE

NOTE: THIS TEMPLATE
IS PRINTED AT 50%
ITS CORRECT SIZE

TO USE, SCALE IT UP 200%
ON A PHOTOCOPIER

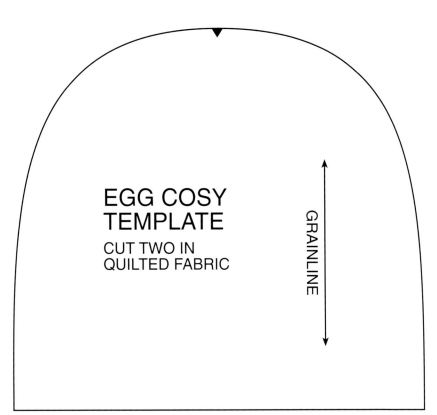

EGG COSY TEMPLATE
CUT TWO IN
QUILTED FABRIC

GRAINLINE

ROMAN GLASS PEG BAG AND BREAKFAST ON THE TERRACE EGG COSY TEMPLATES

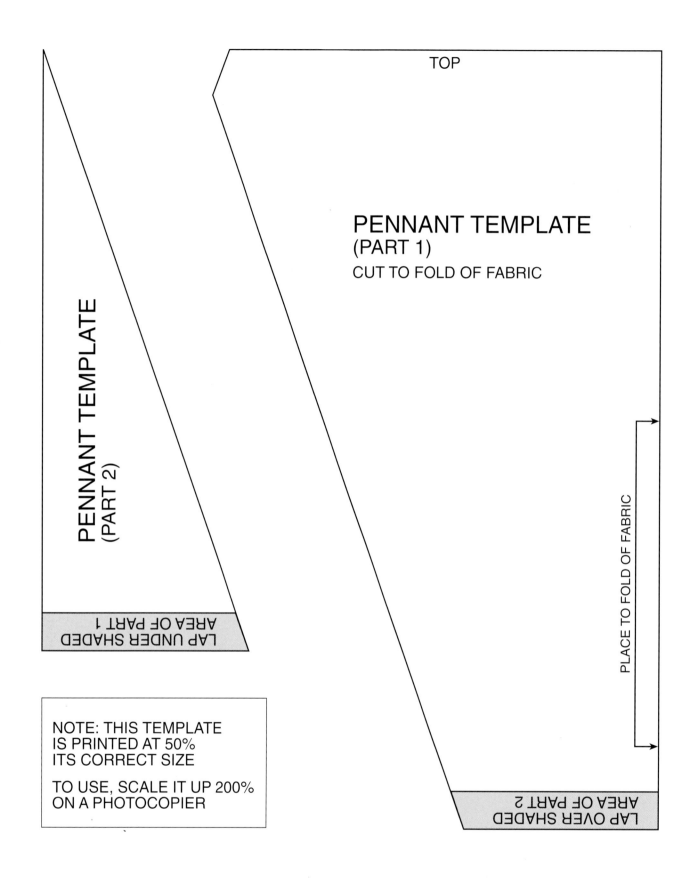

TOP

PENNANT TEMPLATE
(PART 1)
CUT TO FOLD OF FABRIC

PENNANT TEMPLATE
(PART 2)

LAP UNDER SHADED
AREA OF PART 1

PLACE TO FOLD OF FABRIC

LAP OVER SHADED
AREA OF PART 2

NOTE: THIS TEMPLATE
IS PRINTED AT 50%
ITS CORRECT SIZE

TO USE, SCALE IT UP 200%
ON A PHOTOCOPIER

CELEBRATION BANNERS TEMPLATE

STRIPY OVEN MITTS
TEMPLATE

LEAF TEMPLATE

APPLIQUED TABLECLOTH AND NAPKINS TEMPLATE

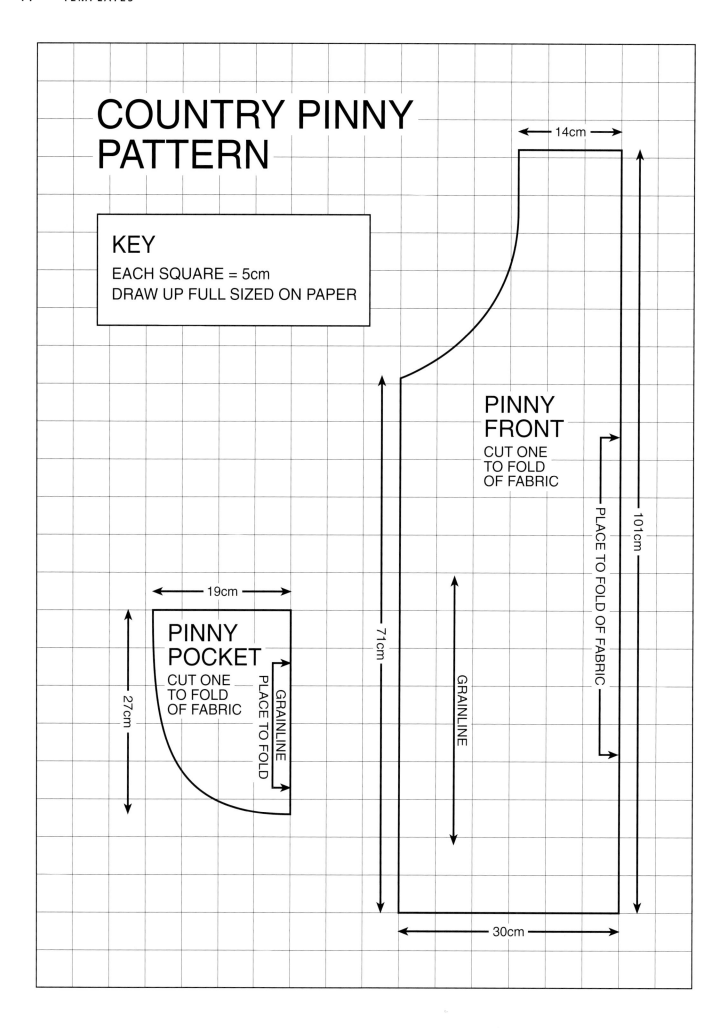

COUNTRY PINNY PATTERN

KEY

EACH SQUARE = 5cm
DRAW UP FULL SIZED ON PAPER

14cm

PINNY FRONT

CUT ONE
TO FOLD
OF FABRIC

PLACE TO FOLD OF FABRIC

101cm

71cm

GRAINLINE

30cm

19cm

PINNY POCKET

CUT ONE
TO FOLD
OF FABRIC

GRAINLINE
PLACE TO FOLD

27cm

STRIPY CUSHION TEMPLATE

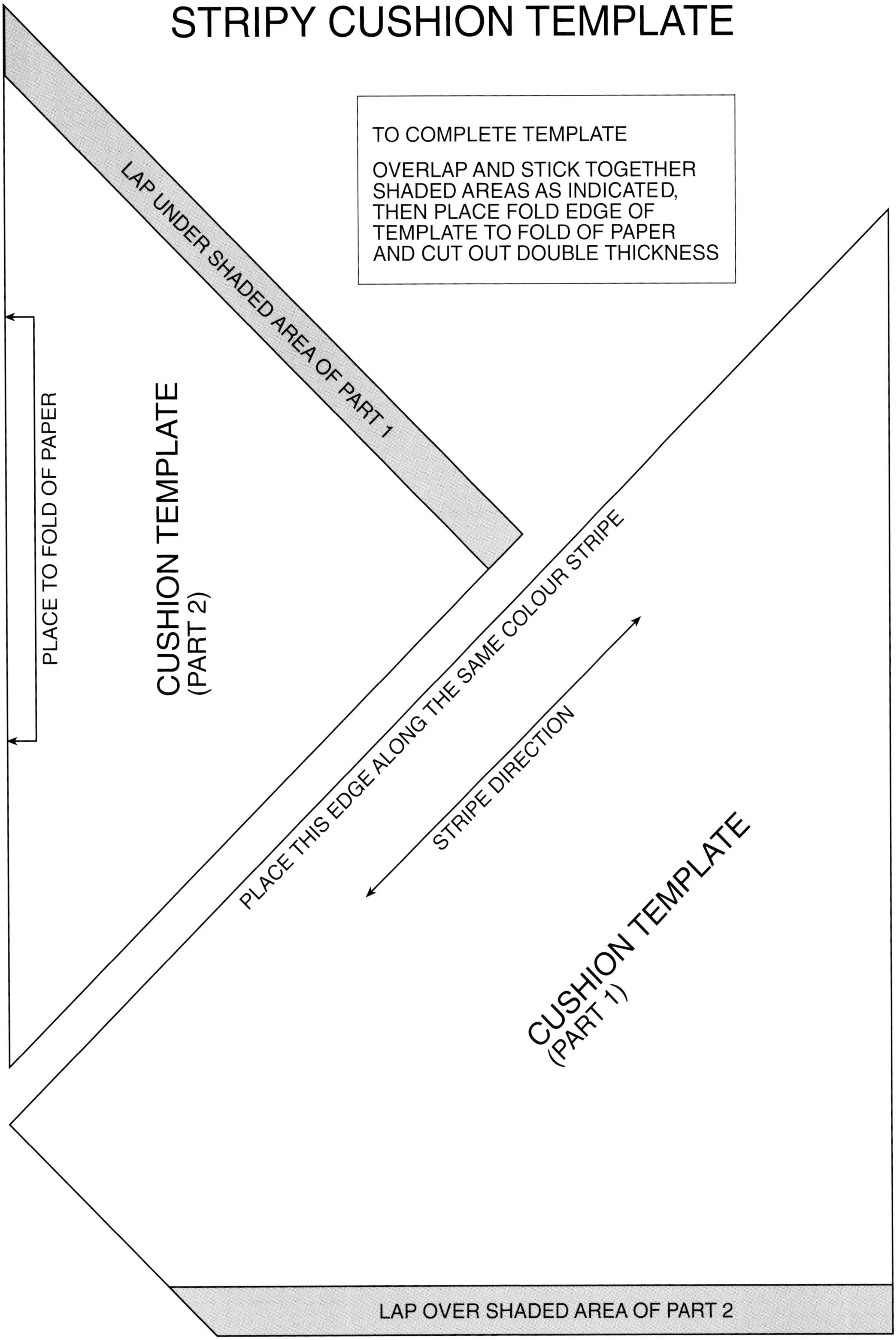

TO COMPLETE TEMPLATE

OVERLAP AND STICK TOGETHER
SHADED AREAS AS INDICATED,
THEN PLACE FOLD EDGE OF
TEMPLATE TO FOLD OF PAPER
AND CUT OUT DOUBLE THICKNESS

LAP UNDER SHADED AREA OF PART 1

PLACE TO FOLD OF PAPER

CUSHION TEMPLATE
(PART 2)

PLACE THIS EDGE ALONG THE SAME COLOUR STRIPE

STRIPE DIRECTION

CUSHION TEMPLATE
(PART 1)

LAP OVER SHADED AREA OF PART 2

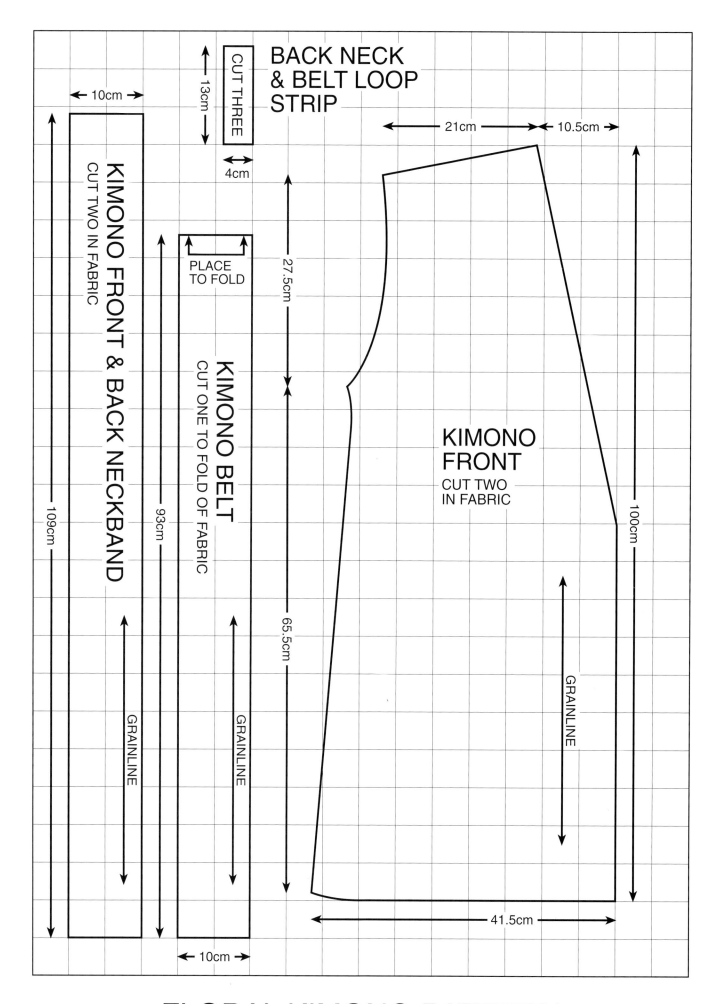

BACK NECK
& BELT LOOP
STRIP

CUT THREE

13cm

4cm

10cm

KIMONO FRONT & BACK NECKBAND
CUT TWO IN FABRIC

109cm

GRAINLINE

PLACE
TO FOLD

KIMONO BELT
CUT ONE TO FOLD OF FABRIC

93cm

GRAINLINE

10cm

27.5cm

65.5cm

21cm

10.5cm

KIMONO
FRONT
CUT TWO
IN FABRIC

100cm

GRAINLINE

41.5cm

FLORAL KIMONO PATTERN

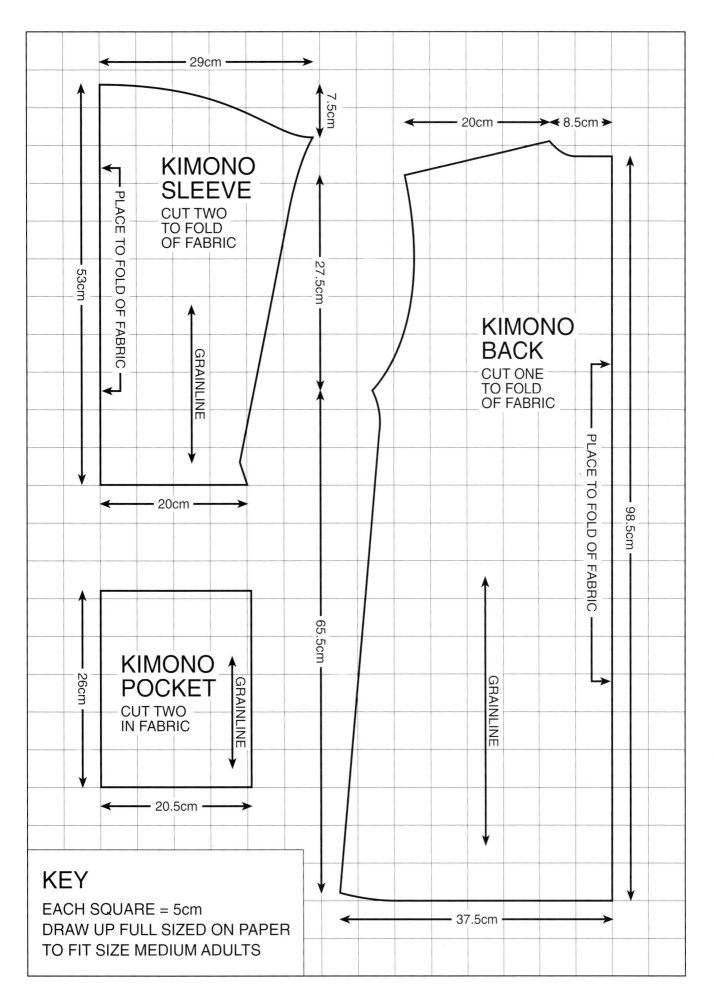

29cm

7.5cm

KIMONO
SLEEVE
CUT TWO
TO FOLD
OF FABRIC

PLACE TO FOLD OF FABRIC

53cm

GRAINLINE

27.5cm

20cm

65.5cm

20cm 8.5cm

KIMONO
BACK
CUT ONE
TO FOLD
OF FABRIC

PLACE TO FOLD OF FABRIC

98.5cm

GRAINLINE

KIMONO
POCKET
CUT TWO
IN FABRIC

26cm

GRAINLINE

20.5cm

37.5cm

KEY

EACH SQUARE = 5cm
DRAW UP FULL SIZED ON PAPER
TO FIT SIZE MEDIUM ADULTS

APPLIQUE
PATCH TEMPLATE

ORIENTAL
CHARACTER
MOTIFS

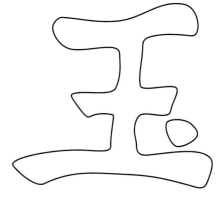

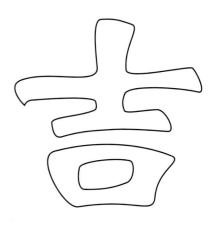

ZEN SHOWER CURTAIN

The Rowan Patchwork and Quilting Collection

Three books in our Patchwork and Quilting range available from
Rowan Stockists and selected book shops

**Patchwork and Quilting
Book Number One
£7.50**

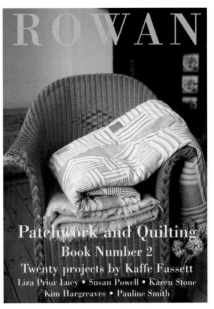

**Patchwork and Quilting
Book Number Two
£9.95**

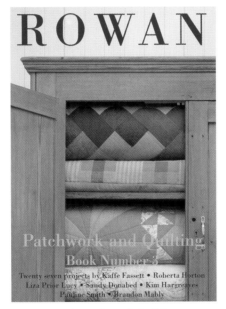

**Patchwork and Quilting
Book Number Three
£10.95**

R O W A N

Green Mill, Holmfirth, West Yorkshire, England
Tel: +44 (0) 1484 681881   Fax: +44 (0) 1484 687920   Internet: www.knitrowan.com   Email: Mail@knitrowan.com

Index